Statistics for the Health Sciences

Statistics
for the
Health Sciences

USING SPSS

Basant K Puri
Research Fellow,
Charing Cross and Westminster Medical School,
University of London, UK

W. B. Saunders Company Ltd
London Philadelphia Toronto Sydney Tokyo

W. B. Saunders Company Ltd 24–28 Oval Road
London NW1 7DX

The Curtis Center
Independence Square West
Philadelphia, PA 19106-3399, USA

Harcourt Brace & Company
55 Horner Avenue
Toronto, Ontario M8Z 4X6, Canada

Harcourt Brace & Company, Australia
30–52 Smidmore Street
Marrickville, NSW 2204, Australia

Harcourt Brace & Company, Japan
Ichibancho Central Building, 22-1 Ichibancho
Chiyoda-ku, Tokyo 102, Japan

A catalogue record for this book is available from the British Library

ISBN 0-7020-1876-7

Typeset by Mackreth Media Services, Hemel Hempstead, Herts
Printed and bound in Great Britain by Hartnolls Ltd, Bodmin, Cornwall

Preface

In this book no prior knowledge on the part of the reader has been assumed and only an elementary knowledge of algebra is required. Accordingly each topic is introduced gently, examples are given and there is extensive use of explanatory diagrams. The emphasis throughout is on understanding the basic principles. Exercises are provided for chapters 1 and 3 to 7, and all chapters end with a summary.

The reader has not been burdened with unnecessary details. For example, the chapter on ANOVA simply explains how, why and when tests based on the F distribution are used. I have assumed that the reader wishing to run an ANOVA test after reading this chapter will do so with a computer statistics package rather than manually. Therefore the text has not been obscured with irrelevant details.

SPSS commands have been included for the statistical tests and graphical plots. Their inclusion will, I hope, encourage those with access to this popular statistics package to run SPSS while, or straight after, reading each chapter.

Basant Puri

Contents

CHAPTER 1

Introduction to statistics

BASIC CONCEPTS

STATISTICS

Definition

The Shorter Oxford English Dictionary defines statistics as:

> *the department of study that has for its object the collection and arrangement of numerical facts or data, whether relating to human affairs or to natural phenomena.*

Statistics can also involve making decisions, predictions and inferences about the populations (see below) from which the data are drawn. This and a further use of the term statistics are illustrated in Example 1.1.

Example 1.1 Suppose we wanted to know the average age of onset of schizophrenia in males. One method of doing this might be to try and find out the age of onset of every single documented case of schizophrenia in males throughout the world, add all these ages together, and then divide by the number of male schizophrenic patients. This would give the average (or mean) age of onset. Clearly, this would be a very long and difficult task to carry out. A more practical method makes use of statistical techniques.

All male patients with schizophrenia can be said to form a **population** – this is the set of all people (or objects etc.) about which information (in this case the average age of onset) is required. The average age of onset of this population is a population **parameter**. A random **sample** taken from this population can be used to estimate the average age of onset. This estimate is a sample **statistic**. That is, a sample statistic can be used to estimate the population parameter, as shown in Figure 1.1. In this diagram statistics can refer to the collection and arrangement of the appropriate data, the sample statistics, and the process of making an inference about population parameters from samples drawn from the population.

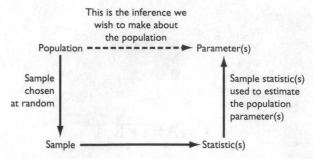

Figure 1.1   The relationship between statistics and parameters

If the procedure in Example 1.1 were repeated with female patients with schizophrenia, we would then have estimates of the average age of onset of both male and female schizophrenic patients. These could then be compared with each other using an appropriate statistical procedure (such as the *t* test described in Chapter 5).

Classification
Descriptive statistics are ways of organizing data or information. Examples include tables, diagrams, graphs and numerically. For instance, the average ages of onset of schizophrenia for males and females (Example 1.1) could be summarized in a bar chart, as in Figure 1.2.

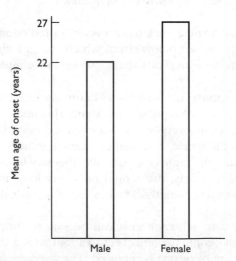

Figure 1.2   An example of descriptive statistics: mean age of onset of schizophrenia

Inferential statistics allow conclusions to be derived from the data. This corresponds to the dotted line at the top of Figure 1.1. An example could be in relation to the data described in Figure 1.2, for which inferential statistical methods (such as the *t* test) have shown that the mean age of onset of schizophrenia in males is significantly earlier than in females.

VARIABLES

Definition
A variable is a quantity or attribute that varies from one member of the population being studied to another. In Example 1.1 the age of onset is the quantity of interest that varies from one member of the population to another. So, in that example, age of onset can be said to be a variable being studied.

Classification
Variables can be qualitative (categorical) or quantitative (numerical). **Qualitative** (categorical) variables refer to attributes that can be separated into categories such that the categories do not have a numerical relationship with each other. Examples include gender (male, female) and eye colour (blue, brown, grey, etc.).

Quantitative (numerical) variables refer to numerically represented data, which can be discrete or continuous. **Discrete** quantitative variables can only take on known fixed values. An example is the daily number of admissions to a hospital ward. The value of this variable can be 0, 1, 2, 3, and so on, but not values in between (such as 1.8 admissions).

Continuous quantitative variables can take on any value within a defined range. An example is body mass. For instance, a person may have a body mass of 56.3 kg, to one decimal place; that is, a mass has been allocated to the range 56.25 to 56.35 kg (exclusive). Figure 1.3 summarizes the classification of variables.

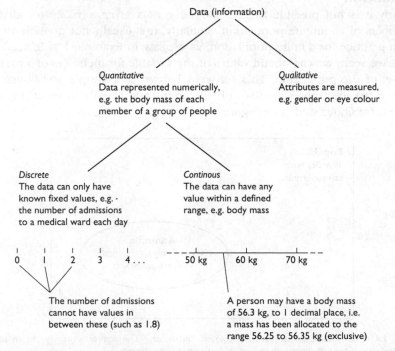

Figure 1.3   Summary of the classification of variables

POPULATIONS

Definition
As already mentioned, a population is the total collection of objects, people or data about which information is needed.

Classification
In Example 1.1 all male patients with schizophrenia can be said to form a population. Since there is a limit to number of such patients, this population is said to be **finite**.

An example of an **infinite** population is the case where the results of repeated throws of two dice are being measured, since in theory the dice could be thrown for ever.

Parameter
A parameter is a summarizing value which describes a population. In Example 1.1 the *actual* mean age of onset of schizophrenia in males is a population parameter.

SAMPLES

Definition
Clearly it is not possible to find the value of a given variable for all the members of an infinite population. Similarly, it is usually not possible to do so in practice for a finite population, as we saw in Example 1.1. Instead, as we have seen, we can obtain values of the variable for members of a part or subset of the population. This subset is known as a sample and is usually chosen to be representative of the population with respect to the variable(s) under study (see Figure 1.4).

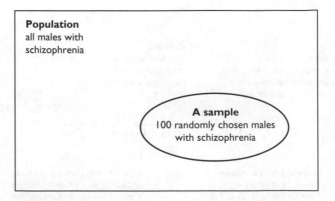

Figure 1.4   The relationship between a population and a sample. A sample is usually chosen to be representative of the population with respect to the variable being studied

Statistic

A statistic is a summarizing value that describes a sample. In Example 1.1 the mean age of onset in a representative randomly chosen sample is a statistic, which can then be used to estimate the value of the corresponding parameter.

NOTATION

English (Roman) letters are generally used to denote sample statistics, while Greek letters are used for population parameters, as shown in Table 1.1.

Table 1.1 Notation: examples of statistics and their corresponding parameters

Statistic	Parameter
$\bar{x}$ (pronounced 'x bar'): sample mean	μ: population mean
s or sd or SD: sample standard deviation	σ: population standard deviation
r: Pearson sample correlation coefficient	ρ: Pearson population correlation coefficient
a: sample intercept of a regression line	α: intercept of a regression line in a population
b: gradient of a sample regression line	β: gradient of a regression line in a population

Variables are conventionally represented by capital italic English letters (e.g. X), while a corresponding small English italic letter (x) is used to represent a value of that variable. For more than one value of the variable, subscripts (x_1, x_2, x_3, and so on) can be used. An estimated value is represented by a hat ($\hat{x}$) and a mean value by a bar ($\bar{x}$).

Other types of notation are explained where necessary in the rest of this book. In general, however, the use of mathematical notation has been kept to a minimum.

USE OF COMPUTERS

Apart from simple calculations, such as working out the mean of a small number of values, most statistical procedures are now carried out using computers. For this reason, details of how to carry out calculations using one of the most popular statistics software packages, SPSS for Microsoft Windows, are given in this book. However, the relevant formulae are briefly mentioned where appropriate, enabling manual calculations to be carried out by those who wish to.

MEASUREMENT SCALES

There are four main types of measurement scale that can be used for different types of data: nominal, ordinal, interval and ratio (see Table 1.2).

Table 1.2 Types of measurement scale

Property	Nominal	Ordinal	Interval	Ratio
Categories mutually exclusive	✓	✓	✓	✓
Categories logically ordered		✓	✓	✓
Equal distance between adjacent categories			✓	✓
True zero point				✓

NOMINAL

A nominal measurement scale is a set of mutually exclusive categories that varies qualitatively but not quantitatively. Examples include gender and eye colour. Numbers may be attached to these categories but do not imply that any one category is higher than another. For example, when measuring gender, 0 may stand for female and 1 for male, but this does not imply that the two categories are unequal.

ORDINAL

An ordinal measurement scale differs from a nominal scale in that the categories are ordered; however, differences between adjacent categories are not equal. Examples include social class and the staging of cancer. Numbers attached to these categories reflect their relative order. For example, social class 1 is higher than social class 3; however, the difference between social classes 1 and 3 is not the same as the difference between social classes 3 and 5 (even though numerically $3-1 = 5-3$). In other words the numbers just give the rank.

The ordinal scale is more informative than the nominal scale.

INTERVAL

An interval scale differs from an ordinal scale in that the differences between adjacent categories are equal; however, there is no true zero point. Examples include the Fahrenheit and Celsius temperature scales. For example, 50°F is a higher temperature than 40°F, and the difference in temperature between 50°F and 40°F is the same as the difference between 25°F and 15°F; however, 50°F is not twice the temperature of 25°F, since 0°F is not absolute zero.

The interval scale is more informative than nominal and ordinal scales.

RATIO

A ratio scale differs from an interval scale in that there is a true zero point. Examples include the measurement of height in metres and the Kelvin temperature scale. For example, not only is the difference in height between 0.5 m and 0.4 m the same as the difference between 0.25 m and 0.15 m, but 0.5 m is twice 0.25 m.

The ratio scale is more informative than the preceding three scales.

SUMMARY

■ Statistics can refer to: the collection and arrangement of data; the procedures for making decisions, predictions and inferences about populations; and summarizing values that describe samples.

■ Descriptive statistics are ways of organizing data while inferential statistics allow conclusions to be derived from the data.

■ Variables can be qualitative (categorical) or quantitative (numerical), and the latter can be discrete or continuous.

■ A parameter is a summarizing value which describes a population.

■ The hierarchy of measurement scales that can be used for different types of data is (least informative first): nominal, ordinal, interval and ratio.

EXERCISE

1. What do you understand by the term statistics?

2. What is the difference between a sample and a population?

3. Define and classify variables.

4. To which type of measurement scale (nominal, ordinal, interval or ratio) do each of the following belong?

   (a) temperature measured in °C
   (b) temperature measured in K
   (c) body mass
   (d) social class
   (e) number of siblings
   (f) religious belief

2

CHAPTER 2

Data presentation

Data can be presented in tables and diagrammatically. These can confer the following advantages over just calculating the numerical summarizing values described in the rest of the book:

▨ They can give an overall picture of the data, which may allow relationships to be discerned and allow one to check if certain assumptions needed for some statistical techniques are met.

▨ A diagram such as a graph may allow an approximate value or range for a statistic to be estimated; for example, a scatter diagram may allow the range for a correlation coefficient to be estimated.

▨ If a mistake has been made in data entry on a keyboard or in using a calculator, resulting in an incorrect value for a statistic or parameter, this may be recognized because of the estimated value from the diagram.

FREQUENCY DISTRIBUTION AND FREQUENCY TABLE

A frequency distribution is a systematic way of arranging data. When displayed in the form of a frequency table, the first column gives possible categories (values) of a qualitative or quantitative variable. The next column gives the frequency with which each category occurs.

Example 2.1 Table 2.1 is a frequency table based on a study of problems with bleeding reported by patients receiving anticoagulation in 688 visits (Ryan *et al.*, 1989). None of the patients was found to suffer from more than one such problem with bleeding.

RELATIVE FREQUENCY

The relative frequency of a variable is the proportion of the total frequency that corresponds to that variable. It is calculated from:

$$\text{Relative frequency} = \frac{\text{Frequency of category}}{\text{Total frequency}} \qquad (2.1)$$

Relative frequencies can be expressed as percentages by multiplying by 100. The sum of all the relative frequencies is always 1 (or 100%). (The sum may differ very slightly from 1 in a table because of rounding errors.)

Table 2.1 Frequency table of problems with bleeding during anticoagulation

Problem	Frequency (number of patients)
Epistaxis	15
Excessive bruising	7
Gastrointestinal bleeding	5
Haematuria	0
Haemoptysis	2
Menorrhagia	0
Oral mucosal bleeding	0
Other	4
Total	33

Example 2.2 The data of Table 2.1 can be converted into the relative frequency table shown in Table 2.2.

Table 2.2 Relative frequency table of the data in Table 2.1

Problem	Relative frequency		
Epistaxis	15/33 = 0.455	or	45.5%
Excessive bruising	7/33 = 0.212	or	21.2%
Gastrointestinal bleeding	5/33 = 0.152	or	15.2%
Haematuria	0/33 = 0	or	0%
Haemoptysis	2/33 = 0.061	or	6.1%
Menorrhagia	0/33 = 0	or	0%
Oral mucosal bleeding	0/33 = 0	or	0%
Other	4/33 = 0.121	or	12.1%
Total	33/33 = 1	or	100%

BAR CHART

A bar chart is suitable for representing the values of a discrete variable; the individual categories in the chart do not touch each other. Figure 2.1 is a bar chart representing the data of Table 2.1.

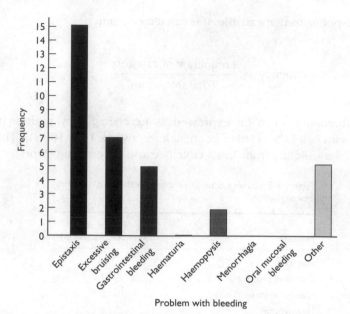

Figure 2.1   A bar chart representing the frequency data of Table 2.1 – problems with bleeding during anticoagulation

It is important, when drawing a bar chart, for the vertical axis to start at zero. If none of the categories has a value of zero, and the vertical axis starts above zero, this can exaggerate any differences between categories and be potentially misleading.

Figure 2.2 is a relative frequency bar chart representing the data of

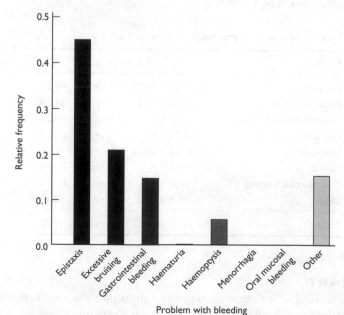

Figure 2.2   A bar chart representing the relative frequency data of Table 2.2

Table 2.2. The length of each bar is directly proportional to the frequency (or relative frequency) of each category.

SPSS for Windows

A bar chart can readily be constructed by SPSS. First the data of Table 2.1 have to be entered in the Newdata spreadsheet.

Define variable: bleeding
Define label: Variable label = Problems with bleeding
Value labels
    1 = epistaxis
    2 = excessive bruising
    and so on
Continue → OK

In the first column of Newdata
    the first 15 cases = 1
    the next 7 cases = 2
    and so on

Then click on Graphics
    Bar
        Simple (Data in Chart are Summaries for groups of cases)

Define
    Category Axis = bleeding
    (Bars represent N of cases)
    OK
→ Bar chart in Chart Carousel

In this bar chart those categories with a count of zero are not shown.
To make the vertical axis start at zero, select Edit in the Chart Carousel
    Chart
        Axis
      - Scale axis
          Select the required range

HISTOGRAM

A histogram can be used when the variable is continuous.

Table 2.3 Haemoglobin levels (g dl^{-1}) for 25 randomly chosen male outpatients

14.7	13.6	15.3	16.3	13.4
14.7	14.9	14.7	16.4	13.7
16.1	15.8	16.1	14.8	15.5
15.2	15.7	16.3	15.8	15.6
15.4	14.3	12.6	14.5	16.2

Example 2.3　Table 2.3 gives the haemoglobin levels found in 25 randomly chosen male outpatients. It is helpful to group the data into a small number of classes that cover successive values, such as:

12.0 to 12.9 g dl^{-1}
13.0 to 13.9 g dl^{-1}
14.0 to 14.9 g dl^{-1}

and so on.

The range covered by each class is called the **class interval**. Figure 2.3 is a histogram of these data. Note that when the class intervals are the same size then the heights of the rectangles equal the class frequencies. As with bar charts, beware of the potential to give a misleading picture if the vertical axis does not start at zero. The histogram can be converted into a relative frequency histogram simply by replacing the vertical axis with a relative frequency axis. Note also that the rectangles touch each other; this is because the variable is continuous.

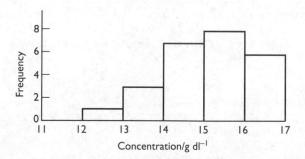

Figure 2.3　*A histogram representing the data of Table 2.3 – haemoglobin levels of 25 randomly chosen male outpatients.* Redrawn from Puri and Tyrer (1992) *Sciences Basic to Psychiatry*, with permission from Churchill Livingstone, Edinburgh, UK.

SPSS for Windows
Select Graphics
　　　Histogram
　　　　　Enter variable
　　　　　OK

FREQUENCY POLYGON

A frequency polygon is derived from a histogram by joining together with straight lines the mid-points of the tops of the rectangles of the histogram. (Again, beware of the potential to mislead if the vertical axis does not begin at zero.) So, for Example 2.3, the frequency polygon shown in Figure 2.4 can be constructed.

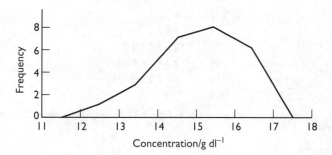

Figure 2.4 A frequency polygon representing the data of Table 2.3 – haemoglobin levels of 25 randomly chosen male outpatients. Redrawn from Puri and Tyrer (1992) Sciences Basic to Psychiatry, with permission from Churchill Livingstone, Edinburgh, UK.

Frequency polygons can be useful when comparing more than one set of data. For example, Figure 2.5 shows the frequency polygon of Figure 2.4 with a superimposed frequency polygon representing the haemoglobin levels of 25 randomly chosen adult female outpatients.

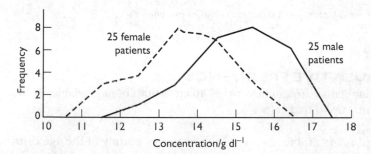

Figure 2.5 The frequency polygon of Fig. 2.4 with a superimposed frequency polygon representing the haemoglobin levels of 25 randomly chosen adult female outpatients. Redrawn from Puri and Tyrer (1992) Sciences Basic to Psychiatry, with permission from Churchill Livingstone, Edinburgh, UK.

SPSS for Windows
Select Graphics
    Line
        Define Simple or Multiple, as appropriate
        OK

STEM-AND-LEAF DIAGRAM

A stem-and-leaf diagram can be used to represent a continuous variable. It is similar to a histogram except that it allows all the individual data to be represented. Figure 2.6 is a stem-and-leaf diagram of the data of Table 2.3. The vertical column of numbers of the left (the stems) represent 12, 13, 14, 15 and 16 g dl^{-1}. All the individual data can then be derived by joining each of the numbers to the right of the stems (the leaves), representing in this case tenths g dl^{-1}, to the corresponding stem.

```
12    6
13    4 6 7
14    3 5 7 7 7 8 9
15    2 3 4 5 6 7 8 8
16    1 1 2 3 3 4
```

Figure 2.6   A stem-and-leaf diagram of the data in Table 2.3 – haemoglobin levels of 25 randomly chosen male outpatients

SPSS for Windows
Statistics
    Summarize
        Explore
        Define variable
            Plots
                Stem-and-leaf
                Continue
                OK

The stem-and-leaf diagram appears in the Output window.

CUMULATIVE FREQUENCY

The cumulative frequency of a given value of a variable is the total frequency up to that value.

Example 2.4   Table 2.4 shows the results of a study of the age distribution of early-onset and late-onset depression in a sample of elderly patients (Burvill *et al.*, 1989). The table also gives the cumulative frequencies. For example, in the third column, 31 = 18 + 13, 44 = 31 + 13, and so on.

Table 2.4 Age distribution of patients with early-onset and late-onset depression

Age (years)	Early-onset		Late-onset	
	Frequency	Cumulative frequency	Frequency	Cumulative frequency
60–64	18	18	5	5
65–69	13	31	5	10
70–74	13	44	11	21
75–79	6	50	12	33
80–84	1	51	11	44
85–89	1	52	6	50

Cumulative frequency data can be represented graphically. The data of Table 2.4 is represented graphically in Figure 2.7, which makes the relationship between early-onset and late-onset depression clearer.

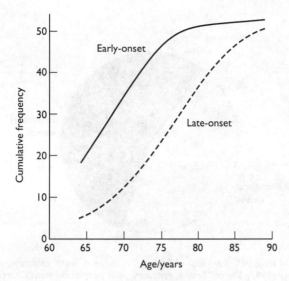

Figure 2.7   Cumulative frequency curves representing the data of Table 2.4 – age distribution of patients with early-onset and late-onset depression. Redrawn from Puri and Tyrer (1992) *Sciences Basic to Psychiatry*, with permission from Churchill Livingstone, Edinburgh, UK.

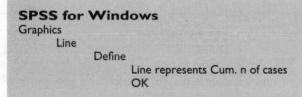

SPSS for Windows
Graphics
     Line
        Define
             Line represents Cum. n of cases
             OK

PIE DIAGRAM

A pie diagram (pie chart) is an alternative to a bar chart. A circle is divided into sectors whose sizes correspond to the proportional frequencies of the categories represented. The frequency proportion of each category is multiplied by 360° to obtain the angle of the corresponding sector.

Example 2.5   Table 2.5 gives the causes of spinal cord compression. The last column shows how to work out the angles for the sectors representing each category. Figure 2.8 is the corresponding pie diagram.

Table 2.5 Causes of spinal cord compression

Cause	Proportion of total	Angle of sector for pie diagram
Extradural	45% (= 0.45)	$0.45 \times 360° = 162°$
Intradural	45%	$0.45 \times 360° = 162°$
Intramedullary	10%	$0.1 \times 360° = 36°$

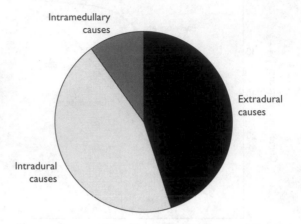

Figure 2.8   Pie chart representing the data of Table 2.5 – causes of spinal cord compression. Redrawn from Puri and Tyrer (1992) *Sciences Basic to Psychiatry,* with permission from Churchill Livingstone, Edinburgh, UK.

SPSS for Windows
Graphics
     Pie
          Define
          OK

PICTOGRAM

In a pictogram the number of times a standard symbol such as a picture is repeated corresponds to the value of each category.

Example 2.6   Table 2.6 gives the annual number of babies born in a hospital over seven years.

Table 2.6 The number of babies born in a hospital over a seven-year period

Year	Number of babies
1	502
2	597
3	648
4	873
5	909
6	964
7	1010

By representing every 100 babies with the symbol shown, the pictogram in Figure 2.9 can be constructed.

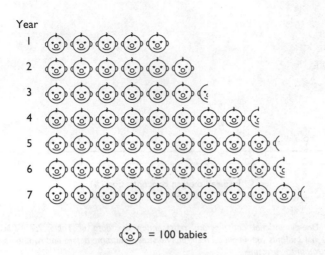

Figure 2.9 *Pictogram representing the data of Table 2.6 – annual number of babies born over a seven-year period*

ONE-DIMENSIONAL DOT DIAGRAM

In this frequency distribution diagram each observation appears as a dot on a calibrated line. Different colours or shading can represent dots from different sets of observations, allowing comparisons to be made visually.

Example 2.7 Table 2.7 shows part of the results of a study of the inspired oxygen concentrations (percentages) in 13 infants with neonatal respiratory distress syndrome before and two hours after the start of negative extrathoracic pressure (Samuels and Southall, 1989).

Table 2.7 Inspired oxygen concentrations (percentages) in 13 infants with neonatal respiratory distress syndrome before and two hours after the start of negative extrathoracic pressure

Before	After 2 hours
40, 60, 100, 100, 100, 100, 60, 100, 100, 100, 100, 100, 100	30, 55, 55, 85, 85, 80, 40, 70, 90, 80, 90, 87, 55

Figure 2.10 is a one-dimensional dot diagram of these results. Where there is more than one observation with the same value, the corresponding dots have been stacked vertically.

BOX-AND-WHISKER PLOT

This is a diagrammatic way of representing the maximum, minimum, and quartiles (including the median) of a skewed distribution. The quartiles are described in the next chapter, where a box-and-whisker plot is shown.

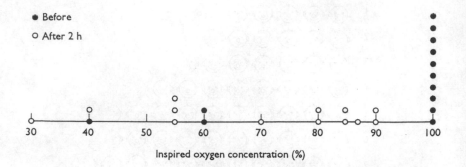

Figure 2.10   One-dimensional dot diagram representing the data of Table 2.7 – inspired oxygen concentrations in 13 infants with neonatal respiratory distress syndrome before and two hours after the start of negative extrathoracic pressure

SCATTER DIAGRAM

A scatter diagram (dot graph) allows data from two continuous variables to be compared visually. Two axes at right angles divide the space into a coordinate system, in which each pair of observations is plotted.

Example 2.8   Table 2.8 shows the elimination half-life of zopiclone and the corresponding serum albumin level for nine cirrhotic patients (after Parker and Roberts, 1983). These data are plotted as a scatter diagram in Figure 2.11. As we will see in Chapter 7, plotting a scatter diagram is useful before calculating the correlation coefficient and linear regression equation of two continuous variables.

Table 2.8 The elimination half-life of zopiclone and corresponding serum albumin levels in nine cirrhotic patients

Patient	Serum albumin (g l^{-1})	Elimination half-life (h)
1	29.2	10.0
2	25.1	11.6
3	27.5	9.2
4	27.5	12.6
5	40.0	6.2
6	42.4	5.3
7	41.7	7.8
8	36.6	7.2
9	42.1	7.8

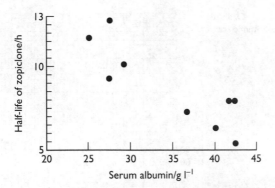

Figure 2.11   Scatter diagram representing the data of Table 2.8 – the elimination half-life of zopiclone and corresponding serum albumin levels in nine cirrhotic patients. Redrawn from Puri and Tyrer (1992) Sciences Basic to Psychiatry, with permission from Churchill Livingstone, Edinburgh, UK.

SPSS for Windows
Graphics
   Scatter
      Define (decide what type of scatter diagram you want (2-D, 3-D, etc.) and which variable should be on the X-axis and which on the Y-axis)
      OK

LINE GRAPHS

A line graph is similar to a scatter diagram, with successive points, relative to the horizontal axis, joined by straight lines. The frequency polygon of Figure 2.4 is an example of a line graph. In a time series, the horizontal axis of the line graph represents time.

SPSS for Windows
Graphics
   Line
      Define
      OK

LOG-LINEAR GRAPH

In this graph one axis, usually the vertical one, has a logarithmic scale, with the other axis being linear. Figure 2.12 shows the appearance of log-linear graph paper. A logarithmic scale is useful for a variable when its range is very large and difficult to represent on a linear axis, or when it is useful to transform its data by taking the logarithms. (One reason for transforming a variable is that this may be a way of making its distribution similar to that of the Normal distribution (see Chapter 4), thereby allowing the application of

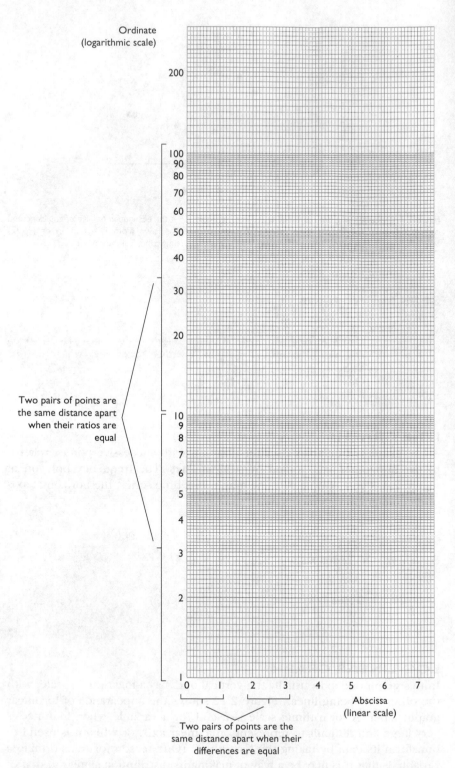

Figure 2.12   Log-linear graph paper. Redrawn from Puri and Tyrer (1992) *Sciences Basic to Psychiatry*, with permission from Churchill Livingstone, Edinburgh, UK.

statistical procedures that assume the values are Normally distributed.) Figure 2.13 is a log-linear graph showing the rates of accidents and serious injury or death in car drivers by age and sex for Great Britain in 1986 (Department of Transport, 1987).

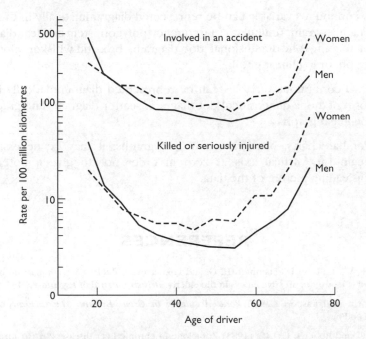

Figure 2.13   Rates of accidents and serious injury or death in car drivers by age and sex for Great Britain in 1986 (Department of Transport, 1987)

SPSS for Windows

A scatter diagram, with one axis being logarithmic and the other linear, can be constructed by transforming the variable that is to be plotted on the logarithmic scale as follows:

Transform
        Compute
                (Define the target variable) = LG10 (original variable)
                OK

This transforms the original variable into its logarithms to base 10. To transform to natural logarithms, use the function LN instead.

SUMMARY

■   Diagrammatic and tabular representations of data can help give an overall picture, show possible relationships, help check the distribution(s), determine an approximate statistical value, and help check for mistakes.

- Discrete variables can be represented diagrammatically in the form of a bar chart, pie diagram, or pictogram.

- A continuous variable can be represented diagrammatically in the form of a histogram, (cumulative) frequency polygon, stem-and-leaf diagram, pictogram, one-dimensional dot diagram, box-and-whisker plot, line graph, or log-linear graph.

- Two continuous variables can be represented diagrammatically in the form of a one-dimensional dot diagram, scatter diagram, line graph, or log-linear graph.

- For bar charts, histograms and line graphs, it may be necessary to begin the vertical axis at zero in order not to give a potentially misleading picture of the data.

REFERENCES

Burvill, P. W., Hall, W. D., Stampfer, H. G. and Emmerson, J. P. (1989) A comparison of early-onset and late-onset depressive illness in the elderly. *British Journal of Psychiatry*, **155**, 673-9.

Department of Transport (1987) *Road Accidents in Great Britain. The Casualty Report*, HMSO, London.

Parker, G. and Roberts, C. J. C. (1983) Zopiclone in chronic liver disease. *British Journal of Clinical Pharmacology*, **16**, 259-65.

Ryan, P. J., Gilbert, M., and Rose, P. E. (1989) Computer control of anticoagulant dose for therapeutic management. *BMJ*, **299**, 1207-9.

Samuels, M. P. and Southall, D. P. (1989) Negative extrathoracic pressure in treatment of respiratory failure in infants and young children. *BMJ*, **299**, 1253-7.

CHAPTER 3

Summarizing data

A data distribution can be summarized by giving both a measure of its location (e.g. mean) and a measure of its dispersion (e.g. standard deviation).

MEASURES OF LOCATION

Measures of central tendency (e.g. the mean) are commonly used as measures of location and attempt to give a value around which a distribution clusters. Quantiles are measures of location that, in addition to a measure of central tendency (the median), also include other values.

MEASURES OF CENTRAL TENDENCY

Arithmetic mean
The arithmetic mean (or average or simply the mean) of a set of numbers is calculated by dividing the sum of the items by the number of items. For a sample with n items ($x_1, x_2, x_3, ..., x_n$):

$$\text{Mean, } \bar{x} = \frac{\Sigma x}{n} \tag{3.1}$$

where Σ stands for 'sum of', and Σx is the sum of all the items (x_1, x_2, x_3, and so on to x_n). Similarly, the population mean, μ, of a population of size N is given by:

$$\mu = \frac{\Sigma x}{N} \tag{3.2}$$

The mean is suitable for use with data measured on *interval* or *ratio* scales, but not nominal or ordinal ones.

Example 3.1 Table 3.1 shows the ages (in years) of 27 inpatients with learning disabilities in a Regional Secure Unit known as the ESU (Puri *et al.,* 1995). Calculate the mean age.

Table 3.1 Ages (in years) of 27 inpatients

22.9	23.3	20.6	22.3	22.6	25.1	47.8	32.8	37.4	20.8	43.0	23.1	32.3	36.0	26.7
28.1	42.9	54.5	63.2	8.9	29.2	43.7	47.2	36.2	31.9	33.6	26.1			

Sum of ages, $\Sigma x = 882.2$ years
Number of patients, $n = 27$
From Equation 3.1, mean age, $\bar{x} = 882.2/27 = 32.7$ years

The main disadvantage of the mean is that it takes all values into account. Therefore it can be unduly influenced by an extreme value so that the measure of central tendency given by the mean may be one around which few or no other actual values exist. Another measure of central tendency, the median, is useful in such a case.

SPSS for Windows
Select Statistics
       Summarize
              Descriptives
              Select Mean in Options
              OK

Median
The median is the middle value of a set of observations ranked in order. If there is an odd number of observations, the median is the middle value. If there is an even number of observations, the median is the arithmetic mean of the two middle values. The median gives a better measure of central tendency than the mean when the distribution is *skewed*, that is when the distribution is asymmetrical (see Figures. 3.4 and 3.5 below).

The median is suitable for use with data measured on *ordinal*, *interval* or *ratio* scales, but not a nominal one. It is often preferred to the mean when some values in a distribution are unknown, as in survival data.

Example 3.2 Calculate the median age for the data in Table 3.1.

There are 27 observations, and so the median is the 14th observation when the ages are ranked in order. Therefore, the median is 31.9 years.

Mode

The mode of a distribution is the value of the observation occurring most frequently. The category or interval occurring most frequently is called the modal category. If an extreme value occurs most frequently then this is the mode, and in this case it could be argued that the mode is not strictly speaking a measure of central tendency.

The mode can be used with all measurement scales. As Example 3.3 illustrates, mode is often not useful with continuous variables.

Example 3.3   Calculate the modal age for the data in Table 3.1.

There are no repeated values in this distribution, and therefore there is no mode.

Example 3.4   Which is the modal category in Table 2.1?

The modal category is the one occurring most frequently: epistaxis.

DISTRIBUTION CURVES

In the frequency polygon of Figure 3.1 there is clearly one mode, and the

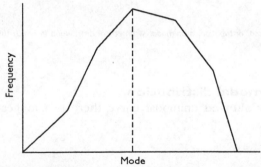

Figure 3.1   A unimodal distribution

distribution is therefore called **unimodal**. A **bimodal** distribution has two modes, a **trimodal** three, and **multimodal** many. In practice, the distribution in Figure 3.2 would be called bimodal because it has two peak values, even though they are not of equal size.

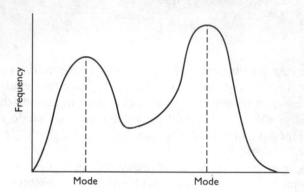

Figure 3.2   A bimodal distribution

Symmetrical unimodal distribution

In these distributions the mean, median and mode are equal. This is shown in Figure 3.3 for the Normal distribution, which is an example of a symmetrical unimodal distribution.

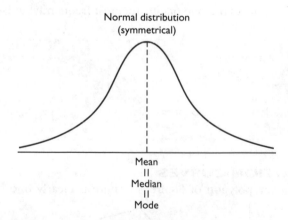

Figure 3.3   The Normal distribution, a unimodal symmetrical distribution in which the mean, median and mode are equal

Skewed unimodal distribution

In a **positively skewed** unimodal curve there is a longer right tail (see Figure 3.4) and:

mode < median < mean

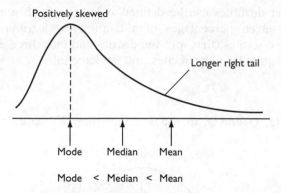

Figure 3.4 A positively skewed unimodal distribution

In a **negatively skewed** unimodal curve there is a longer left tail (see Figure 3.5) and:

mean < median < mode

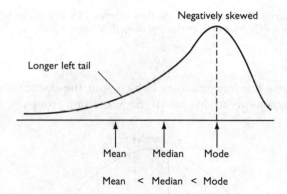

Figure 3.5 A negatively skewed unimodal distribution

QUANTILES

We have just seen how the median splits a distribution into two equal parts, as shown in Figure 3.6.

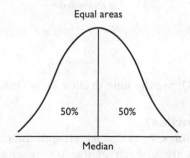

Figure 3.6 The median

Similarly, other quantiles can be defined as being cut off points below or above which given percentages of a continuous distribution lie. They include the two tertiles (that split the distribution into three groups), three quartiles, four quintiles, nine deciles, and 99 percentiles.

Quartiles

In Figure 3.7, Q_1, Q_2 and Q_3 are the three quartiles. Q_2 is equal to the median.

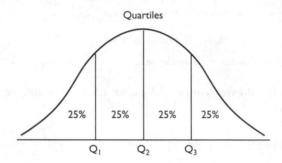

Figure 3.7   *The quartiles. Q_1, Q_2 and Q_3 are the three quartiles. 25% of values lie below Q_1 (the first quartile), between Q_1 and Q_2, between Q_2 and Q_3, and above Q_3 (the third quartile)*

Quintiles

Figure 3.8 shows the four quintiles, which split the distribution such that 20% of the observations are in each of the 5 resulting groups.

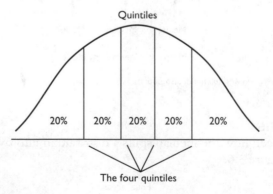

Figure 3.8   *The quintiles*

Deciles

In Figure 3.9, D_1 to D_9 are the nine deciles. D_5 is equal to the median.

Percentiles (centiles)

There are 99 percentiles, P_1 to P_{99}, which split the distribution such that 1% of the observations are in each of the 100 resulting groups. The middle percentile, P_{50}, is equal to the median.

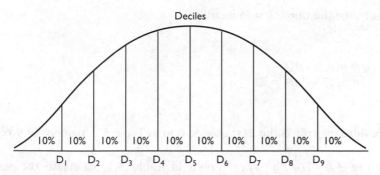

Figure 3.9   The deciles. D_1 to D_9 are the nine deciles. The fifth decile, D_5, is equal to the median

Calculation

The n observations are ranked in increasing order from the first to the nth. The kth quantile is then calculated by interpolating between the two observations adjacent to the qth, where q is given by:

$$q = k(n + 1)/Q \tag{3.3}$$

where Q = the number of groups into which the quantiles divide the distribution (e.g. $Q = 10$ for deciles, 100 for percentiles, and so on).

Example 3.5   For the ages shown in Table 3.1, calculate the first and third quartiles.

Table 3.2 gives the ages ranked in ascending order. Considering Equation 3.3, quartiles divide the distribution into four equal groups, and so $Q = 4$. The total number of observations, $n = 27$.

Table 3.2 Ages (in years) from Table 3.1 ranked in ascending order

8.9	20.6	20.8	22.3	22.6	22.9	23.1	23.3	25.1	26.1	26.7	28.1	29.2	31.9	32.3
32.8	33.6	36.0	36.2	37.4	42.9	43.0	43.7	47.2	47.8	54.5	63.2			

For the first ($k = 1$) quartile,

$$q = k(n + 1)/Q$$
$$= 1(27 + 1)/4 = 28/4 = 7$$

Since q is an exact integer, the 7th value in Table 3.2 is the first quartile, namely 23.1 years.

Similarly, for the third ($k = 3$) quartile,

$$q = k(n + 1)/Q$$
$$= 3(27 + 1)/4 = 21$$

So the third quartile is the 21st observation in Table 3.2, namely 42.9 years.

Example 3.6   For the ages shown in Table 3.1, calculate the second decile.

Deciles divide the distribution into 10 equal groups, and so $Q = 10$. The total number of observations, $n = 27$. For the second ($k = 2$) decile,

$$q = k(n + 1)/Q$$
$$= 2(27 + 1)/10 = 5.6$$

The two observations adjacent to the qth are therefore the 5th and 6th ones, which from Table 3.2 are 22.6 and 22.9 years, respectively. Since $q = 5.6 = 5 + 0.6$, the required second decile is interpolated as being at 6 tenths (0.6) of the interval between the 5th and 6th observations.

(6th observation) – (5th observation) = 22.9 − 22.6 = 0.3 years

Therefore

$$\text{Second decile} = (5\text{th observation}) + (0.3)(0.6)$$
$$= 22.6 + 0.18$$
$$= 22.78 \text{ years}$$

SPSS for Windows
Select Statistics
      Summarize
           Frequencies
           In Statistics select Quartiles for quartiles, or select Cut points for ___
           equal groups (and state the number of equal groups, e.g. 5 for quintiles,
           10 for deciles, etc.), or select Percentiles and state the cut off point(s)
           below which the stated percentage of the distribution lies
           OK

MEASURES OF DISPERSION

Measures of location alone, while helpful as statistical descriptions, do not describe the extent of dispersion of a distribution. Considered on their own, they can be misleading. For example, in Figure 3.10 the patients with a given disease have the same mean plasma concentration of a certain hormone as do normal controls. However, the patients have a greater variation or dispersion of values of the concentration.

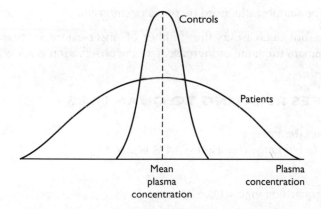

Figure 3.10   Two distributions having the same mean and difference dispersions

The measures of dispersion described here are the range, measures relating to quantiles, and the standard deviation and variance.

RANGE

The range is the difference between the smallest and largest values in a distribution:

$$\text{range} = (\text{largest value}) - (\text{smallest value}) \tag{3.4}$$

The range can be used with data that are measured with *interval* or *ratio* scales.

Example 3.7   Calculate the range for the ages shown in Table 3.1.

Range = (largest value) − (smallest value)
      = 63.2 − 8.9
      = 54.3 years

The range has the following disadvantages:

- It does not give any information about the dispersion of values lying between the smallest and the largest.

- It can be unduly influenced by one extreme value.

- It does not decrease as the number of observations increases; it can only remain the same or increase if a new observation is added.

MEASURES RELATING TO QUANTILES

Interquartile range

The interquartile range (see Figure 3.11) is given by:

$$\text{Interquartile range} = Q_3 - Q_1 \tag{3.5}$$

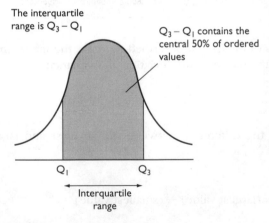

Figure 3.11   *The interquartile range*

Example 3.8 Calculate the interquartile range for the ages shown in Table 3.1.

From Equation 3.5,

$$\text{Interquartile range} = Q_3 - Q_1$$
$$= 42.9 - 23.1 \quad \text{(from Example 3.5)}$$
$$= 19.8 \text{ years}$$

SPSS for Windows
Select Statistics
       Summarize
              Frequencies
              In Statistics select Quartiles
              OK

Output: subtract the value of the 75.00 Percentile (Q_3) from that of the 25.00 Percentile (Q_1)

Semi-interquartile range (quartile deviation)

The semi-interquartile range (see Figure 3.12) is given by:

$$\text{Semi-interquartile range} = \frac{Q_3 - Q_1}{2}$$

(3.6)

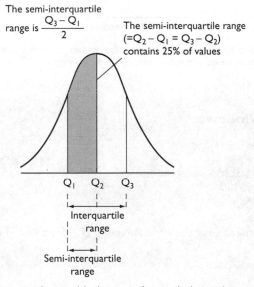

The semi-interquartile range is $\frac{Q_3 - Q_1}{2}$

The semi-interquartile range ($= Q_2 - Q_1 = Q_3 - Q_2$) contains 25% of values

Q_1 Q_2 Q_3

Interquartile range

Semi-interquartile range

Figure 3.12   The semi-interquartile range (also known as the quartile deviation)

SPSS for Windows
Select Statistics
       Summarize
              Frequencies
              In Statistics select Quartiles
              OK

Output: subtract the value of the 75.00 Percentile (Q_3) from that of the 25.00 Percentile (Q_1) and divide the result by 2

10 to 90 percentile range (interdecile range)

The 10 to 90 percentile (interdecile) range (see Figure 3.13) contains the central 80% of ordered values and is given by:

$$10 \text{ to } 90 \text{ percentile range} = P_{90} - P_{10} = D_9 - D_1 \qquad (3.7)$$

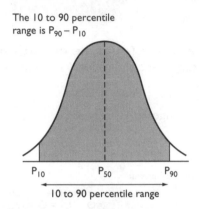

Figure 3.13 *The 10 to 90 percentile (interdecile) range contains the central 80% of ordered values. It is also equal to $D_9 - D_1$, hence the alternative name of interdecile range*

SPSS for Windows
Select Statistics
    Summarize
        Frequencies
        In Statistics select Percentiles
        Add 10 and 90
        OK

Output: subtract the value of the 10.00 Percentile (P_{10}) from that of the 90.00 Percentile (P_{90})

Skewed distributions and box-and-whisker plots (boxplots)

The mean and standard deviation (described below) are usually given as summarizing measures of central tendency and dispersion, respectively, for distributions. However, when a distribution is skewed it can be more useful to give the median as the measure of central tendency and a measure relating to quantiles (often the interquartile range or the 10 to 90 percentile range) as the measure of dispersion.

These can be plotted in a box-and-whisker plot (or boxplot), whose features are shown in Figure 3.14. The box-length represents the interquartile range and the whiskers extend to the smallest and largest observations, excluding outliers and extreme values. Any outliers and extreme values can be indicated using symbols such as ○ and *, respectively.

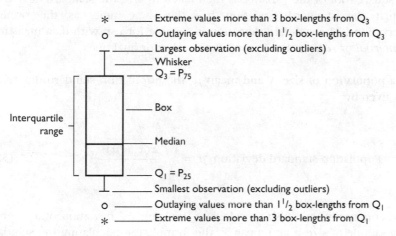

Figure 3.14 *Features of a box-and-whisker plot (boxplot) – not to scale*

Example 3.9 Create a box-and-whisker plot of the ages shown in Table 3.1.

The values of the median, and first and third quartiles have previously been calculated, and there are no outliers or extreme values as defined above. The required box-and-whisker plot is shown in Figure 3.15.

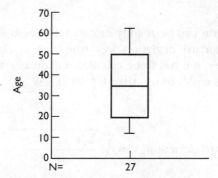

Figure 3.15 *A box-and-whisker plot (boxplot) of the ages shown in Table 3.1*

SPSS for Windows
Graphics
    Boxplot
    Choose Data in Chart are Summaries of separate variables or Summaries for groups of cases, as appropriate
    Define
        OK

STANDARD DEVIATION

The standard deviation is based on deviations from the mean, which are squared, summed, and averaged (divided by N or $n-1$) to give the variance. The square root of the variance is then taken to give the standard deviation, so that the standard deviation has the same units as the original observations. The standard deviation is suitable for use with data measured on *interval* or *ratio* scales, but not nominal or ordinal ones.

For a population of size N and mean μ, the population standard deviation, σ, is given by:

$$\text{Population standard deviation, } \sigma = \sqrt{\frac{\Sigma(x - \mu)^2}{N}} \tag{3.8}$$

More commonly, we wish to calculate the standard deviation of a sample. For a sample of size n and mean $\bar{x}$, the formula for calculating the standard deviation is similar to Equation 3.8, except that we divide by $(n-1)$ rather than just n. This reason for this is beyond the scope of this book. So the sample standard deviation, s, is given by:

$$\text{Sample standard deviation, } s = \sqrt{\frac{\Sigma(x - \bar{x})^2}{n-1}} \tag{3.9}$$

The standard deviation can be readily calculated using a statistics computer program or the standard deviation key (the one marked σ_{n-1} on most calculators). However, if it has to be calculated manually, then the following equivalent formula is easier to use than Equation 3.9:

$$\text{Sample standard deviation, } s = \sqrt{\frac{\Sigma(x^2) - (\Sigma x)^2/n}{n-1}} \tag{3.10}$$

Example 3.10   Calculate the standard deviation of the ages shown in Table 3.1.

In Table 3.3 the ages are represented by x. From this table we have:

$\Sigma x = 882.2$ (omitting units)
$\Sigma x^2 = 32\,558.70$
$n = 27$

Substituting into Equation 3.10,

Sample standard deviation = square root of $[(32\,558.70 - (882.2)^2 /27)/26]$
= square root of 143.60
= 12.0 years (to one decimal place)

(Note that in future Examples, as in Example 3.10, units will be omitted during the calculations, and the answer usually given with a degree of accuracy comparable with the original data.)

Table 3.3 Ages (in years) from Table 3.1 represented by x, and calculation of x^2, Σx, and Σx^2

x	x^2
8.9	79.21
20.6	424.36
20.8	432.64
22.3	497.29
22.6	510.76
22.9	524.41
23.1	533.61
23.3	542.89
25.1	630.01
26.1	681.21
26.7	712.89
28.1	789.61
29.2	852.64
31.9	1017.61
32.3	1043.29
32.8	1075.84
33.6	1128.96
36.0	1296.00
36.2	1310.44
37.4	1398.76
42.9	1840.41
43.0	1849.00
43.7	1909.69
47.2	2227.84
47.8	2284.84
54.5	2970.25
63.2	3994.24
882.2	32 558.70

SPSS for Windows
Select Statistics
  Summarize
    Descriptives
    Select Std. deviation in Options
    OK

VARIANCE

The variance is the square of the standard deviation. As with the standard deviation, the variance is suitable for use with data measured on *interval* or *ratio* scales, but not nominal or ordinal ones. The formulae required are:

$$\text{Population variance, } \sigma^2 = [\Sigma(x - \mu)^2]/N \tag{3.11}$$

$$\text{Sample variance, } s^2 = [\Sigma(x - \bar{x})^2]/(n-1) \tag{3.12}$$

For manual calculations, the equivalent formula to that in Equation 3.10 can be used:

$$\text{Sample variance, } s^2 = \frac{\Sigma(x)^2 - (\Sigma x)^2/n}{n-1} \tag{3.13}$$

As for the standard deviation, the variance has the advantage of using all the observations in its calculation. However, the units of the variance are the square of those of the observations.

Example 3.11   Calculate the variance of the ages shown in Table 3.1.

Carrying out the calculations shown in Example 3.10, but not taking the square root, sample variance = 143.6 years^2.

SPSS for Windows
Select Statistics
  Summarize
    Descriptives
    Select Variance in Options
    OK

SUMMARY

▪   A data distribution can be summarized by giving both a measure of its location and a measure of its dispersion.

■ Measures of location include measures of central tendency (including the mean, median and mode) and quantiles.

■ The (arithmetic) mean is the average value of a distribution and can be used for data measured on at least an interval scale.

■ The median is the middle value of a set of observations ranked in order and can be used for data measured on at least an ordinal scale.

■ The mode of a distribution is the value of the observation occurring most frequently and can be used with all measurement scales.

■ In a symmetrical unimodal distribution the mean, median and mode are equal.

■ In a positively skewed unimodal curve there is a longer right tail and mode < median < mean.

■ In a negatively skewed unimodal curve there is a longer left tail and mean < median < mode.

■ Quantiles are cut-off points that split a continuous distribution into equal groups.

■ Measures of dispersion include the range, measures relating to quantiles, and the standard deviation and variance.

■ The range is the difference between the smallest and largest values in a distribution and can be used for data measured on at least an interval scale.

■ The interquartile range is the difference between the third and first quartiles; the semi-quartile range is half the interquartile range.

■ The 10 to 90 percentile (interdecile) range is the difference between the 90th and 10th (per)centiles, or equivalently, between the ninth and first deciles.

■ For a skewed distribution it can be more useful to give the median and interquartile or 10 to 90 percentile range rather than the mean and standard deviation.

■ The median and interquartile range can be plotted in a box-and-whisker plot (or boxplot).

■ The standard deviation of a distribution is based on deviations from the mean, has the same units as the original observations, and can be used for data measured on at least an interval scale.

■ The variance is the square of the standard deviation, has units that are the square of those of the observations, and can be used for data measured on at least an interval scale.

EXERCISE

1 Define three measures of central tendency.

2 What are quantiles? Give two examples.

3 Sketch curves representing (a) a symmetrical unimodal distribution, and (b) a negatively skewed distribution. Indicate the approximate location of three measures of central tendency on each curve.

4 Define the range.

5 Define the interquartile range.

6 Draw an annotated diagram of a box-and-whisker plot.

7 How do the standard deviation and variance differ?

8 How does the calculation of a sample standard deviation differ from that of a population standard deviation?

9 For the data in Table 2.3 (haemoglobin levels for 25 randomly chosen male outpatients), calculate the following:

(a) mean   (e) second decile (D_2)
(b) median   (f) interquartile range
(c) mode   (g) standard deviation
(d) range   (h) variance.

REFERENCE

Puri, B. K., Lekh, S. K., and Treasaden, I. H. (1995) A comparison of patients admitted to two regional secure units: one for those of normal intelligence and one for those with learning disabilities. *Medicine, Science and the Law* (in press).

CHAPTER 4

Probability and probability distributions

A knowledge of probability and probability distributions is important in order to understand the remaining chapters of this book.

CLASSICAL PROBABILITY

BASIC FORMULA

Suppose a die is thrown. Since there is an equal chance that any of its six faces may land uppermost, the chance that any given face, say a 'six', may land uppermost is 1 in 6 (see Figure 4.1).

Figure 4.1 One throw of a die. The probability of throwing a 'six' is 1/6

Let the probability of an event E occurring be denoted by $P(E)$. If E can occur in n different ways out of a total of N likely possible ways, then

$$P(E) = \frac{n}{N} \tag{4.1}$$

This is shown for the throw of a die in Figure 4.2.

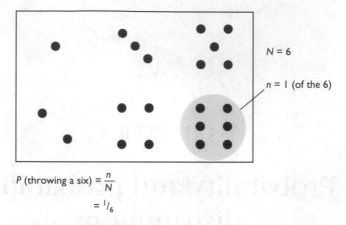

$$P \text{ (throwing a six)} = \frac{n}{N}$$
$$= \text{}^1/_6$$

Figure 4.2   Applying the formula P(E) = n/N to one throw of a die

PROBABILITY OF ZERO

Suppose we try to calculate the probability of throwing a 'seven' (see Figure 4.3).

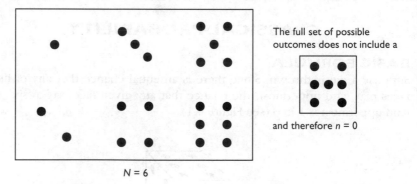

Figure 4.3   The set of possible outcomes of throwing a die does not include a 'seven'

Since there is no possibility of throwing a 'seven', $n = 0$. So,

$$P(\text{throw} = 7) = n/N$$
$$= 0/6$$
$$= 0$$

In general, a probability of 0 implies that an event **never** occurs.

PROBABILITY OF ONE

Suppose we try to calculate the probability of throwing a 'one', 'two', 'three', 'four', 'five' or 'six' (see Figure 4.4).

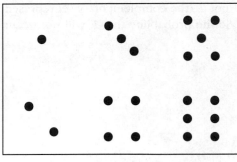

The full set of possible outcomes includes each of 'one' , 'two', 'three', 'four', 'five', and 'six', and no other possibility and therefore $n = 6$

$N = 6$

Figure 4.4   Probability of one

In this case a 'one', 'two', 'three', 'four', 'five' or 'six' will be thrown with one throw of the die, and there is no other possibility. So $n = 6$ and $N = 6$. Therefore:

$$P(\text{throw} = 1, 2, 3, 4, 5 \text{ or } 6) = n/N$$
$$= 6/6$$
$$= 1$$

In general, a probability of 1 implies that an event **always** occurs.

PROBABILITY RANGE

From the above it follows that the probability of an event E occurring can have a minimum value of 0 (implying it never occurs) and a maximum value of 1 (implying it always occurs). In general, the range a probability can take is given by:

$$0 \leqslant P(E) \leqslant 1 \tag{4.2}$$

COMPLEMENTARY EVENTS

Figure 4.5 is a Venn diagram in which an event E can occur in n ways. This is out of a total of N equally likely possible ways, represented by the

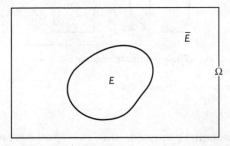

Figure 4.5   Complementary events in the universal set

universal set Ω. Therefore, 'not-E', the complementary set represented by $\bar{E}$, can occur in $(N-n)$ ways. So the probability that E will *not* occur, $P(\bar{E})$, is given by:

$$P(\bar{E}) = (N-n)/N$$
$$= 1-n/N$$

But, $P(E) = n/N$. Therefore:

$$P(\bar{E}) = 1-P(E)$$

or,

$$P(E) + P(\bar{E}) = 1 \qquad (4.3)$$

So, the sum of the probabilities that an event will occur and that it will not occur is equal to 1.

MUTUALLY EXCLUSIVE EVENTS

Events are said to be mutually exclusive if no two can happen together. For example, throwing a 'one' and throwing a 'two' with one throw of a die are mutually exclusive events because if a 'one' is thrown then the die cannot simultaneously show a 'two' as the uppermost face, and vice versa (see Figure 4.6).

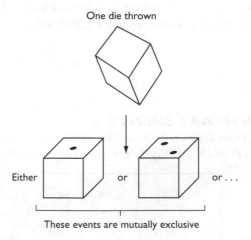

Figure 4.6   *Mutually exclusive events: throwing a die*

Similarly, when a coin is tossed, the two possible resulting events – throwing a head or a tail – are mutually exclusive (see Figure 4.7).

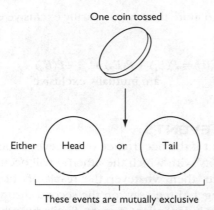

One coin tossed

Either Head or Tail

These events are mutually exclusive

Figure 4.7   Mutually exclusive events: tossing a coin

It can be shown that when two events, E_1 and E_2, are mutually exclusive, the probability that one or the other will occur equals the sum of their probabilities:

$$P(E_1 \text{ or } E_2) = P(E_1) + P(E_2), \text{ where } E_1 \text{ and } E_2 \text{ are mutually exclusive}$$

(4.4)

For example, if a die is thrown (see Figure 4.8):

$$P(\text{throw} = 5 \text{ or } 6) = P(\text{throw} = 5) + P(\text{throw} = 6)$$
$$= 1/6 + 1/6$$
$$= 1/3$$

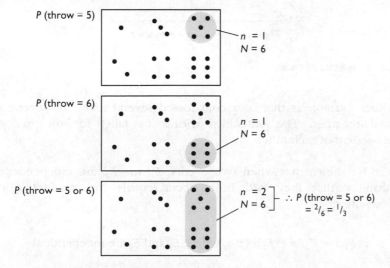

P (throw = 5)

$n = 1$
$N = 6$

P (throw = 6)

$n = 1$
$N = 6$

P (throw = 5 or 6)

$\left. \begin{array}{l} n = 2 \\ N = 6 \end{array} \right]$ $\therefore P$ (throw = 5 or 6)
$= {}^2/_6 = {}^1/_3$

Figure 4.8   Sum of probabilities of mutually exclusive events

This rule also applies to more than two mutually exclusive events:

$$P(E_1 \text{ or } E_2 \text{ or } \dots E_n) = P(E_1) + P(E_2) + \dots + P(E_n)$$
$$\text{where } E_1, E_2, \dots, E_n \text{ are mutually exclusive}$$

(4.5)

INDEPENDENT EVENTS

Events are independent if the occurrence of one event does not in any way influence the probability with which the other(s) will occur. For instance, if a die is thrown twice, then whatever the result of the first throw, the probability of throwing a 'three', say, on the second throw remains 1/6. So these two throws are independent events. Similarly, when two dice are thrown together, the result of each does not affect the result of the other (see Figure 4.9).

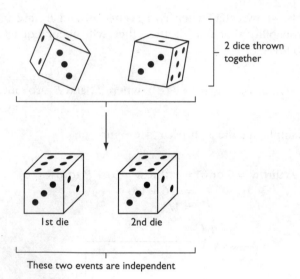

Figure 4.9   Independent events: throwing two dice

Another example is that of a coin tossed several times, or several coins tossed together. The outcomes (heads or tails) for the tosses are independent of each other.

It can be shown that when two events, E_1 and E_2, are independent, the probability that they will both occur equals the product of their probabilities:

$$P(E_1 \text{ and } E_2) = P(E_1)P(E_2), \text{ where } E_1 \text{ and } E_2 \text{ are independent}$$

(4.6)

For example, in the case of two throws of a die, or the throw of two dice together (see Figure 4.10),

$$P(\text{throw} = 6 \text{ and } 6) = P(\text{throw} = 6) \times P(\text{throw} = 6)$$
$$= 1/6 \times 1/6$$
$$= 1/36$$

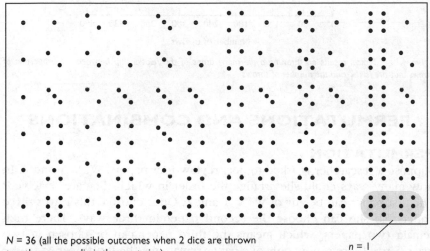

$N = 36$ (all the possible outcomes when 2 dice are thrown together or one die is thrown twice) $n = 1$

$\therefore$ probability $= {}^{n}/_{N} = {}^{1}/_{36}$

Figure 4.10   Product of probabilities of independent events

This rule also applies to more than two independent events:

$$P(E_1 \text{ and } E_2 \text{ and } \dots E_n) = P(E_1)P(E_2) \dots P(E_n)$$
$$\text{where } E_1, E_2, \dots, \text{ and } E_n \text{ are independent} \tag{4.7}$$

LARGE NUMBERS OF TRIALS

While the probability of throwing a 'six', say, with a die is 1/6, this does not imply that in a trial of 6 throws one, and only one, of these throws will be a 'six'. However, the greater the number of throws, the more closely, in general, will the proportion of these throws that are 'sixes' approach 1/6, as shown in Figure 4.11. Similarly, the greater the number of times a coin is tossed, the nearer, in general, does the proportion of heads approach 1/2.

In general, when a trial or experiment is repeated a large number of times, in the long run the relative frequency of a given event approaches the probability of that event occurring.

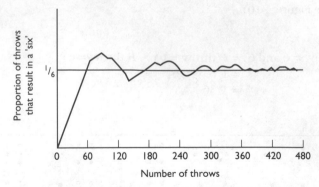

Figure 4.11   Typical results on throwing a die many times of the relationship between the proportion of throws that are 'sixes' and the number of throws

PERMUTATIONS AND COMBINATIONS

PERMUTATIONS

Suppose a researcher is asked to peer-review four papers, W, X, Y and Z. In how many ways could she arrange the order in which they are reviewed? The first paper can be any of W, X, Y and Z. Once chosen, this leaves three papers, so she can choose the second paper in three ways. There then remain two papers, which means the third paper can be chosen in two ways. Since there is now only one paper remaining, the fourth paper can be chosen in just one way. So overall the number of permutations of the four papers is

$$4 \times 3 \times 2 \times 1 = 24$$

These 24 permutations are shown in Table 4.1.

Table 4.1 The permutations of four objects (W, X, Y and Z)

WXYZ	XWYZ	YWXZ	ZWXY
WXZY	XWZY	YWZX	ZWYX
WYXZ	XYWZ	YXWZ	ZXWY
WYZX	XYZW	YXZW	ZXYW
WZXY	XZWY	YZXW	ZYWX
WZYX	XZYW	YZWX	ZYXW

In general, the number of permutations of n objects out of a total of n objects is given by the factorial of n, denoted as $n!$, where:

$$n! = n(n-1)(n-2)(n-3)\ldots1 \tag{4.8}$$

Example 4.1   Calculate 7!

$$7! = 7 \times 6 \times 5 \times 4 \times 3 \times 2 \times 1$$
$$= 5040$$

Suppose the researcher asked to peer-review four papers (W, X, Y and Z) finds she only has time to assess two of them on a given occasion. What is the total number of ways of assessing two papers from four, paying attention to the order in which they are reviewed? The first paper can be any of W, X, Y and Z. Once chosen, this leaves three papers, so she can choose the second paper in three ways. So the total number of ways of assessing two papers from four, paying attention to the order in which they are chosen, is:

$$4 \times 3 = 12$$

These 12 permutations are shown in Table 4.2.

Table 4.2 The permutations of two objects from four (W, X, Y and Z)

WX	XW	YW	ZW
WY	XY	YX	ZX
WZ	XZ	YZ	ZY

This is called a permutation of 2 objects from 4 and is written as $^4P_2$.

In general, the number of permutations of r objects out of a total of n objects is given by:

$$^nP_r = n(n-1)(n-2)(n-3)\ldots(n-r+1)$$

or

$$^nP_r = n!/(n-r)! \tag{4.9}$$

Example 4.2   In how many ways can three objects be chosen from five, paying attention to the order in which they are chosen?

We have $r = 3$ and $n = 5$, and we want $^5P_3$. From Equation 4.9:

$$^5P_3 = 5!/(5-3)!$$
$$= 5!/2!$$
$$= 5 \times 4 \times 3$$
$$= 60$$

COMBINATIONS

Combinations differ from permutations in that the order in which objects are chosen is not important in combinations; what is of importance is just the combination of objects chosen.

Again, suppose the researcher asked to peer-review four papers (W, X, Y and Z) finds she only has time to assess two of them on a given occasion. Let us further suppose that the order in which the papers are assessed is not important to her. That is, while WX and XW would count as two permutations, they would only count as one combination, and so on. In how many ways can she pick two papers from four papers regardless of order? The number of combinations of two objects from four, written as $^4C_2$, is calculated as follows. Since each combination consists of two objects, it follows that the number of ways they can be arranged is 2!, that is, 2. Therefore,

$$2! \times {}^4C_2 = \text{number of permutations}$$
$$\therefore \quad 2! \times {}^4C_2 = {}^4P_2$$
$$\therefore \quad {}^4C_2 = 6$$

These six combinations are shown in Table 4.3 (in which WX could equally be written as XW, WY as YW, and so on; that is, order is not important).

Table 4.3 The combinations of two objects from four (W, X, Y and Z)

WX	XY
WY	XZ
WZ	YZ

Consider the number of ways r objects can be picked from n objects regardless of order, ^nC_r. Each of these combinations consists of r objects, which can therefore be arranged in $r!$ ways. So, in general:

$$r! \, {}^nC_r = {}^nP_r$$
$$= n!/(n-r)!$$

$$\therefore \quad {}^nC_r = \frac{n!}{r!(n-r)!} \tag{4.10}$$

It should be noted that ^nC_r is also conventionally denoted as:

$$\binom{n}{r}$$

Example 4.3   In how many ways can three objects be chosen from five, regardless of order?

We have $r = 3$ and $n = 5$, and we want $^5C_3$. From Equation 4.10:

$$
\begin{aligned}
^5C_3 &= 5!/[3!(5-3)!] \\
&= 5!/(3!2!) \\
&= 5 \times 4/2 \\
&= 10
\end{aligned}
$$

FACTORIAL OF ZERO

Sometimes the use of Equations 4.9 and 4.10 involves 0! The value to assign to the factorial of zero can be obtained by considering ^nC_n. Since there is only one way of picking n objects from n objects regardless of order, it follows that:

$$
\begin{aligned}
^nC_n &= 1 \\
\therefore \quad n!/[n!(n-n)!] &= 1 \\
\therefore \quad n!/[n!0!] &= 1 \\
\therefore \quad 0! &= 1
\end{aligned}
$$

This is taken as the definition of 0!

DISCRETE PROBABILITY DISTRIBUTIONS

BERNOULLI TRIAL

A Bernoulli trial is a trial or experiment that has two and only two alternative outcomes. An example is tossing a coin, since there are just two possible outcomes: heads or tails. Similarly, throwing a 'six' with a die; here the two possible outcomes are: 'six' and 'not-six'. Again, if the sex of a child is assumed only to take on two sexes, then this is another example.

The term 'success' is often used to refer to one of the two outcomes. This does not necessarily mean that the alternative, the 'failure' is not wanted, although often this is the case. For instance, throwing a 'six' with a die may be defined as a 'success' and may in fact be the desired result.

Let the probability of success be p, that is $P(\text{success}) = p$. Then, applying Equation 4.3, we have

$$
\begin{aligned}
P(\text{failure}) &= 1 - P(\text{success}) \\
&= 1 - p
\end{aligned}
\qquad (4.11)
$$

BINOMIAL DISTRIBUTION

Suppose n independent Bernoulli trials, in each of which the probability of success, p, remains the same, are carried out. By independent we mean that the outcome of any given trial does not affect the outcome of any other. If X is the total number of successes, then X is said to follow a binomial distribution with parameters (n, p). This can be written more neatly as:

$$X \sim B(n, p)$$

To illustrate this distribution, the case of tossing a coin is now considered.

Example 4.4 If a fair coin is tossed n times, what is the probability distribution of the number of heads when (a) $n = 0$, (b) $n = 1$, (c) $n = 2$ and (d) $n = 3$?

There are just two alternative outcomes when a coin is tossed, so each toss is a Bernoulli trial.

We are interested in the number of heads, and we will call the outcome 'head' a success.

Let $P(\text{head}) = p$. Since this is a fair coin:

$$P(\text{head}) = P(\text{tail}) = p$$

But, from Equation 4.3:

$$P(\text{head}) + P(\text{tail}) = 1$$

Therefore:

$$p = \tfrac{1}{2}$$

Each time the coin is tossed, the result does not affect the result of any other toss. Moreover, the probability of a success, $\tfrac{1}{2}$, remains the same for each trial. Therefore the number of heads follows a binomial distribution:

$$\text{number of heads} \sim B(n, \tfrac{1}{2})$$

(a) $n = 0$

If there are no tosses of the coin then there is only one possibility for the number of heads:

$$\text{number of heads} = 0$$

This possibility is certain and so carries a probability of 1:

$$P(\text{number of heads} = 0) = 1$$

(b) $n = 1$

If the coin is tossed once, the result could be a head or tail, each of which can occur with a probability of $\frac{1}{2}$:

$$P(\text{number of heads} = 0) = \frac{1}{2}$$
$$P(\text{number of heads} = 1) = \frac{1}{2}$$
$$\text{Sum of probabilities} = 1$$

This is the required probability distribution for $n = 1$, and is shown graphically in Figure 4.12.

The sum of all the probabilities in a probability distribution is 1.

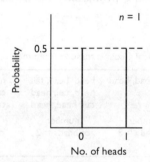

Figure 4.12   Probability distribution for B($1, \frac{1}{2}$); tossing a coin once. Redrawn from Puri and Tyrer (1992) *Sciences Basic to Psychiatry*, with permission from Churchill Livingstone, Edinburgh, UK.

(c) $n = 2$

If the coin is tossed twice there are 4 possible events, shown in Table 4.4. Since each of the four events is equally likely:

$$P(\text{number of heads} = 0) = \frac{1}{4}$$
$$P(\text{number of heads} = 1) = 2/4 = \frac{1}{2}$$
$$P(\text{number of heads} = 2) = \frac{1}{4}$$
$$\text{Sum of probabilities} = 1$$

Table 4.4 The four possible events if a coin is tossed twice

Total of four events	head, head	head, tail tail, head	tail, tail
	number of heads = 2	number of heads = 1	number of heads = 0
Frequency distribution	1	2	1

This probability distribution is shown graphically in Figure 4.13.

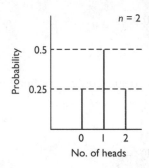

Figure 4.13   Probability distribution for B(2, ½); tossing a coin twice. Redrawn from Puri and Tyrer (1992) *Sciences Basic to Psychiatry*, with permission from Churchill Livingstone, Edinburgh, UK.

(d) $n = 3$

If the coin is tossed three times there are eight possible events, shown in Table 4.5. The corresponding probability distribution is shown graphically in Figure 4.14.

Table 4.5 The eight possible events if a coin is tossed three times

Total of eight events	head, head, head	head, head, tail head, tail, head tail, head, head	head, tail, tail tail, head, tail tail, tail, head	tail, tail, tail
Frequency distribution	number of heads = 3 1	number of heads = 2 3	number of heads = 1 3	number of heads = 0 1

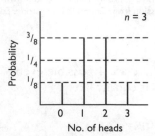

Figure 4.14   Probability distribution for B(3, ½); tossing a coin three times. Redrawn from Puri and Tyrer (1992) *Sciences Basic to Psychiatry*, with permission from Churchill Livingstone, Edinburgh, UK.

Pascal's triangle

The frequency distributions in Example 4.4 can readily be obtained from Pascal's triangle, shown in Figure 4.15. In this triangle of numbers each line begins and ends with 1 and each middle number is the sum of the two numbers immediately adjacent to it on the preceding line. Thus, the first four lines of Pascal's triangle give the frequency distributions for $n = 1, 2, 3$ and 4, respectively, in Example 4.4.

n	Frequency distribution	Total
0	I	I
I	I I	2
2	I 2 I	4
3	I 3 3 I	8
4	I 4 6 4 I	16
5	I 5 10 10 5 I	32
6	I 6 15 20 15 6 I	64
7	I 7 21 35 35 21 7 I	128
⋮	⋯	⋮
n		2^n

Figure 4.15   Pascal's triangle

Binomial distribution when $p \neq \frac{1}{2}$

The probability of success is p and the probability of failure is $(1-p)$ (see Equation 4.11). If, in n independent trials, the number of successes is x, then the number of failures is $(n-x)$.

Applying Equation 4.7 (the product rule for independent events):

Probability of a *specific* series of x successes occurring
by chance $= p^x(1-p)^{n-x}$

Therefore the overall probability of x successes is the product of this term and the number of ways in which x objects can be chosen from n, regardless of order. The latter is simply ^nC_x. So:

$$P(x \text{ successes}) = {^nC_x}\, p^x(1-p)^{n-x} \tag{4.12}$$

The numbers corresponding to ^nC_x are also given by Pascal's triangle, although clearly as n increases it becomes cumbersome to use Figure 4.15, and so it is easier to use Equation 4.10 except when n is small.

Example 4.5   What is the probability distribution for the number of 'sixes' thrown in six throws of a die?

We have:

n = number of trials = 6
p = P(throwing a six) = 1/6

Let X be the number of 'sixes' thrown. Then:

$X \sim B(6, 1/6)$

Using Equation 4.12, and calculating to 3 decimal places:

$P(X = 0) = {}^6C_0 \, (1/6)^0(5/6)^6 = 0.335$
$P(X = 1) = {}^6C_1 \, (1/6)^1(5/6)^5 = 0.402$
$P(X = 2) = {}^6C_2 \, (1/6)^2(5/6)^4 = 0.201$
$P(X = 3) = {}^6C_3 \, (1/6)^3(5/6)^3 = 0.054$
$P(X = 4) = {}^6C_4 \, (1/6)^4(5/6)^2 = 0.008$
$P(X = 5) = {}^6C_5 \, (1/6)^5(5/6)^1 = 0.001$
$P(X = 6) = {}^6C_6 \, (1/6)^6(5/6)^0 = 0.000$

(The sum of these probabilities is 1.)

This probability distribution is shown graphically in Figure 4.16. (Note that unlike Figures 4.12 to 4.14, the distribution is not symmetrical since p and $(1-p)$ are no longer equal.)

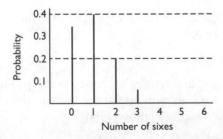

Figure 4.16   Probability distribution for B(6, 1/6); the number of 'sixes' when a die is thrown six times

Mean and variance

Using calculus, it can be shown that the mean and variance of the binomial distribution, $B(n, p)$, are given by:

Mean = np (4.13)

Variance = $np(1-p)$ (4.14)

Example 4.6 What are the mean and variance for the number of 'sixes' thrown in six throws of one die in Example 4.5?

Mean number of 'sixes' thrown in six throws = np
$$= 6(1/6)$$
$$= 1$$

Variance $= np(1 - p)$
$$= 6(1/6)(5/6)$$
$$= 5/6$$

POISSON DISTRIBUTION

The Poisson distribution can be considered to be a special case of the binomial distribution, $B(n, p)$, in which n tends to infinity, p tends to zero (that is, the event is rare), and np is finite. (In reality the Poisson distribution is not just an approximation to the binomial distribution but has its own existence.) The Poisson distribution can be used in situations in which the following criteria are fulfilled:

- events occur randomly in time or space (length, area or volume)

- the events are independent

- two or more events cannot take place simultaneously

- the mean number of events per given unit of time or space is constant.

An example of rare independent events in time that can be modelled using the Poisson distribution is death from certain causes taking place independently and randomly in a given population (Figure 4.17).

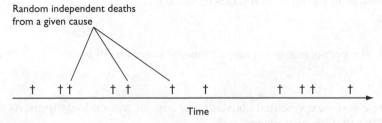

Figure 4.17 An example of rare independent events in time that can be modelled using the Poisson distribution

An example of rare independent events in space that can be modelled using the Poisson distribution is the number of a given type of cells in dilute solution per unit area on a microscope slide, as shown in Figure 4.18.

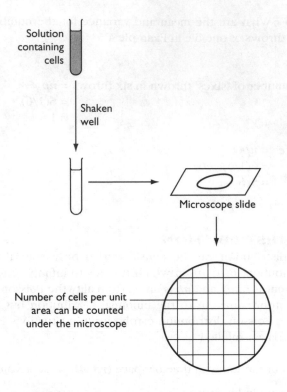

Figure 4.18   An example of rare independent events in space that can be modelled using the Poisson distribution

Let $\mu = np$, where μ is the mean number of events per unit of time or space. Therefore, $p = \mu/n$.

Rewriting p as μ/n in Equation 4.12 for $B(n, p)$, that is, $B(n, \mu/n)$, it can be shown that in the limit, as n tends to infinity:

$$P(x \text{ events in a given unit of time or space}) = e^{-\mu}\mu^x/x! \qquad (4.15)$$

where e is the exponential constant and base of natural logarithms; its value is 2.7183 to 4 decimal places.

A convenient abbreviation for writing the statement that the random variable X follows a Poisson distribution with parameter μ (defined as above) is:

$$X \sim \text{Poisson}(\mu)$$

Example 4.7 If the daily number of emergency admissions to a radiotherapy and oncology unit is 2 and follows a Poisson distribution, what is the probability that on a given day the number of such admissions will be (a) 0, (b) 1 and (c) > 1?

The mean number of emergency admissions, $\mu = 2$ day^{-1}.

Let X be the number of daily emergency admissions. We are told the daily emergency admissions follow a Poisson distribution, therefore:

$X \sim$ Poisson (2)

(a) $X = 0$
From Equation 4.15, and working to 4 decimal places:

$$P(X = 0) = e^{-2}2^0/0!$$
$$= 0.1353$$

(b) $X = 1$

$$P(X = 1) = e^{-2}2^1/1!$$
$$= 0.2707$$

(c) $X > 1$
Since:

$$P(X = 0) + P(X = 1) + P(X = 2) + P(X = 3) + P(X = 4) + \ldots = 1$$

then

$$P(X = 0) + P(X = 1) + P(X > 1) = 1$$

Therefore:

$$P(X > 1) = 1 - P(X = 0) - P(X = 1)$$
$$= 1 - 0.1353 - 0.2707$$
$$= 0.594 \text{ (to 3 decimal places)}$$

Graphical representation
Figures 4.19(a) to (c) show the Poisson distributions for $\mu = 1$, 2 and 5, respectively. As μ increases, the probability distribution becomes more

symmetrical and flatter. Note also that since the sum of all the probabilities is 1, the sum of the lengths of the lines in each of these graphs is also 1.

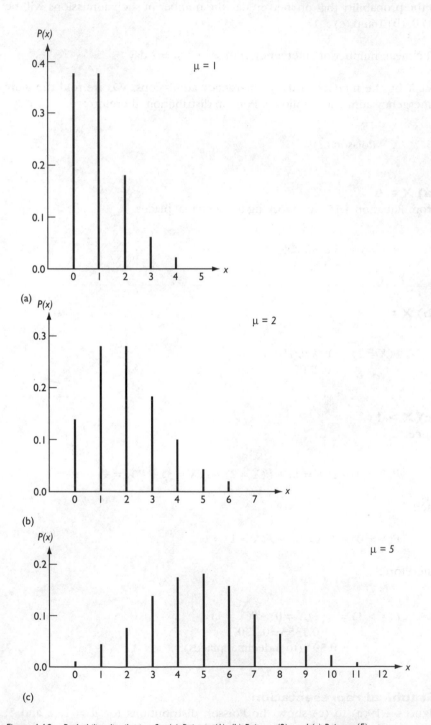

Figure 4.19   Probability distribution for (a) Poisson (1), (b) Poisson (2), and (c) Poisson (5)

Mean and variance

It can be shown that the mean and variance of the Poisson distribution, Poisson (μ), are given by:

$$\text{Mean} = \mu \qquad (4.16)$$

$$\text{Variance} = \mu \qquad (4.17)$$

The equivalence of the mean and variance of a distribution can be a useful indicator when deciding whether a Poisson distribution is appropriate.

Example 4.8 What is the variance for the number of emergency admissions in Example 4.17?

From Equation 4.17:

$$\text{Variance} = 2 \text{ day}^{-2}$$

CONTINUOUS PROBABILITY DISTRIBUTIONS

PROBABILITY HISTOGRAM

While a discrete probability distribution can be represented as a bar chart, as in Figure 4.19(a), it can also be represented as a probability histogram. The sum of the lengths of bars in the bar chart form must come to 1 (since the sum of all the probabilities is 1). For this reason, the area under a probability histogram is also 1. This is demonstrated in Figure 4.20, which is a probability histogram based on Figure 4.19(a).

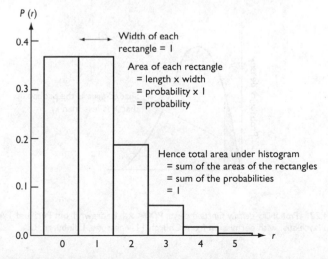

Figure 4.20 Probability histogram representing Poisson (1). Redrawn from Puri and Tyrer (1992) Sciences Basic to Psychiatry, with permission from Churchill Livingstone, Edinburgh, UK.

PROBABILITY DENSITY FUNCTION

The random variable, X say, is continuous in a continuous probability distribution; the latter can therefore be represented graphically as a continuous curve rather than as a probability histogram. The properties of this curve, known as a probability density function, are shown in Figure 4.21. The shaded area in this diagram is $P(x_1 < X < x_2)$. Since the area representing any given value of X is infinitesimally small, the shaded area is also equal to $P(x_1 \leq X \leq x_2)$.

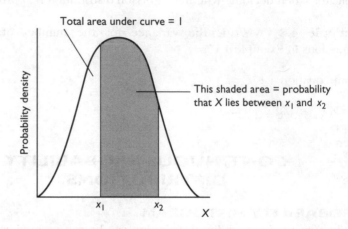

Figure 4.21   Properties of a probability density function curve

In Figure 4.22 the shaded area is $P(X < x_1)$, which is the same as $P(X \leq x_1)$.

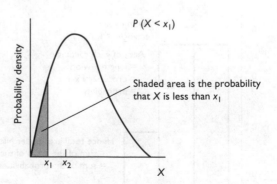

Figure 4.22   Probability density function curve: $P(X < x_1)$. Redrawn from Puri and Tyrer (1992) Sciences Basic to Psychiatry, *with permission from Churchill Livingstone, Edinburgh, UK.*

Similarly, Figure 4.23 shows $P(X > x_2)$, which is the same as $P(X \geq x_2)$.

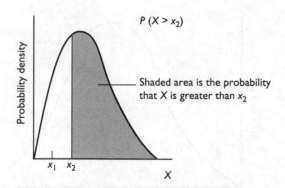

Figure 4.23   Probability density function curve: P(X > x₂). Redrawn from Puri and Tyrer (1992) Sciences Basic to Psychiatry, with permission from Churchill Livingstone, Edinburgh, UK.

NORMAL DISTRIBUTION

Suppose we were to measure the heights, to the nearest 10 cm, of 1000 men chosen at random from a given population. The resulting data could be displayed in the form of a histogram showing the relative frequency, as in Figure 4.24.

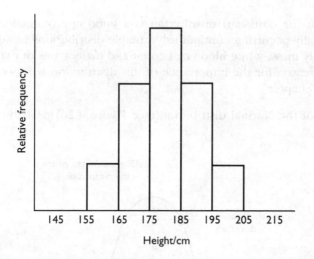

Figure 4.24   Histogram of relative frequency of heights of 1000 men

From this histogram it is clear that the distribution is unimodal and approximately symmetrical. The total area under the histogram is 1. If the height measurements were made increasingly accurate with an increasingly larger sample, the relative frequency histogram could be redrawn with increasingly smaller class intervals, until eventually the curve shown in Figure 4.25 would result.

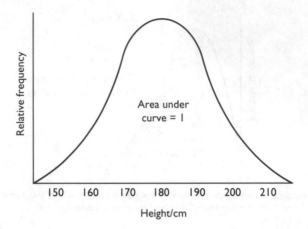

Figure 4.25   Curve of relative frequency of heights of men

This curve approximates to the probability distribution known as the Normal distribution. (In this book the word *normal*, when referring to this distribution, is given an initial capital letter in order to distinguish it from the more common meaning of the word.)

The Normal (or Gaussian) distribution is a good approximation to many other naturally occurring continuously variable distributions besides height, such as body mass, white blood cell count and many types of experimental error. The reason for the importance of this distribution will become clear in the next chapter.

Properties of the Normal distribution (see Figure 4.26) probability density

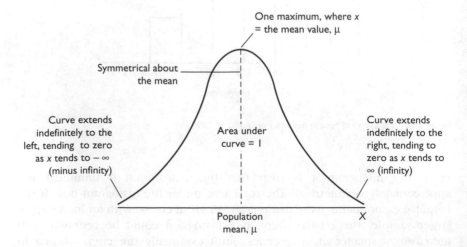

Figure 4.26   Properties of the Normal distribution

function curve include the following:

- it is unimodal

- it is continuous

- it is symmetrical about its mean

- its mean, median and mode are all equal

- the area under the curve is 1

- the curve tends to zero as the variable moves in either direction from the mean.

If X is a random variable that is Normally distributed, with mean μ, and variance σ^2, then the function, $f(x)$, describing the probability density function of X is given by:

$$f(x) = \frac{1}{\sigma\sqrt{2\pi}}\, e^{-((x-\mu)^2/2\sigma^2)} \qquad (4.18)$$

From Equation 4.18 it can be seen that, since e and π are constants, a given Normal distribution is described completely by its mean (μ) and variance (σ^2) (or standard deviation (σ)).

A convenient abbreviation for writing the statement that the random variable X follows a Normal distribution with mean μ and variance σ^2 is:

$$X \sim N(\mu, \sigma^2)$$

Changes in the mean

When the mean of a Normal distribution increases, the whole curve shifts horizontally to the right, as shown in Figure 4.27.

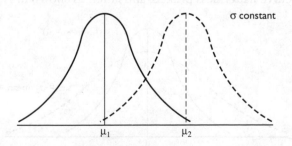

σ constant

Figure 4.27 *Effect on Normal distribution curve of an increase in the mean.* $N(\mu_1, \sigma^2)$ *and* $N(\mu_2, \sigma^2)$, $\mu_2 > \mu_1$

Conversely, a decrease in the mean shifts the Normal distribution curve to the left, as shown in Figure 4.28.

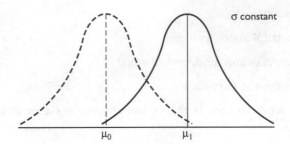

Figure 4.28   *Effect on Normal distribution curve of a decrease in the mean.* $N(\mu_1, \sigma^2)$ *and* $N(\mu_0, \sigma^2)$, $\mu_0 < \mu_1$

Changes in the standard deviation

When the standard deviation of a Normal distribution decreases, the whole curve becomes taller, more peaked, and thinner, as shown in Figure 4.29.

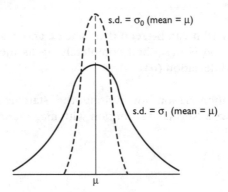

Figure 4.29   *Effect on Normal distribution curve of a decrease in the standard deviation.* $N(\mu, \sigma_1^2)$ *and* $N(\mu, \sigma_0^2)$, $\sigma_0 < \sigma_1$

Conversely, an increase in the standard deviation makes the Normal distribution curve flatter, less peaked, and fatter, as shown in Figure 4.30.

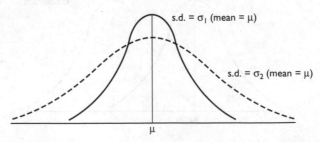

Figure 4.30   *Effect on Normal distribution curve of an increase in the standard deviation.* $N(\mu, \sigma_1^2)$ *and* $N(\mu, \sigma_2^2)$, $\sigma_2 > \sigma_1$

Areas under the curve

For the probability density function of a Normal distribution $N(\mu, \sigma^2)$, the area enclosed by

$$x = \mu - \sigma \quad \text{and} \quad x = \mu + \sigma$$

is 68.27% of the total area under the curve (Figure 4.31).

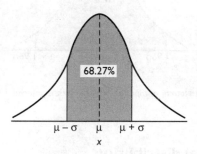

Figure 4.31   Area under the Normal distribution enclosed by the interval one standard deviation either side of the mean

Similarly, the interval 2 standard deviations either side of the mean encloses 95.45% of the total area, while the interval 3 standard deviations either side of the mean encloses 99.73% of the total area (Figure 4.32).

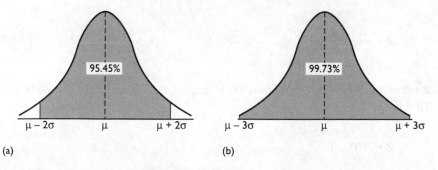

Figure 4.32   Area under the Normal distribution enclosed by the interval (a) two standard deviations either side of the mean and (b) three standard deviations either side of the mean

Since Figures. 4.31 and 4.32 represent probability density functions, they can be expressed as probabilities, as follows. For $X \sim N(\mu, \sigma^2)$:

$$P(\mu - \sigma < X < \mu + \sigma) = 0.6827$$
$$P(\mu - 2\sigma < X < \mu + 2\sigma) = 0.9545$$
$$P(\mu - 3\sigma < X < \mu + 3\sigma) = 0.9973$$

A particularly important range is that corresponding to a probability of 0.95, as is discussed in the next chapter (Figure 4.33):

$$P(\mu - 1.96\sigma < X < \mu + 1.96\sigma) = 0.95$$

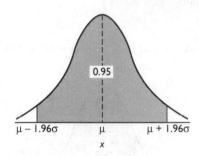

Figure 4.33   Area under the Normal distribution enclosed by the interval 1.96 standard deviations either side of the mean

Standard Normal distribution

As we have seen, if $X \sim N(\mu, \sigma^2)$, a change in the value of μ or σ leads to a change in the corresponding probability density function curve. Determining specific areas under this curve is made easier by first transforming X to a *standard Normal variate*, Z, and then using a table of areas under the curve for Z.

If $X \sim N(\mu, \sigma^2)$, then the standard Normal variate Z is obtained from:

$$Z = \frac{X - \mu}{\sigma} \tag{4.19}$$

Z follows a Normal distribution with mean $(\mu) = 0$ and variance $(\sigma^2) = 1$. That is:

$$Z \sim N(0, 1)$$

The function $\phi(z)$, describing the probability density function of Z, is given by:

$$\phi(z) = \frac{1}{\sqrt{2\pi}}\, e^{-z^2/2} \tag{4.20}$$

(Equation 4.20 can be derived from Equation 4.18 by replacing x with z, and substituting $\mu = 0$ and $\sigma = 1$.)

The value of z is simply the number of standard deviations by which the variable on the horizontal scale differs from the mean. So we can make a direct comparison of the horizontal scale used for the standard Normal distribution (the z-scale) and that used for any Normal distribution (the x-scale), as shown in Figure 4.34.

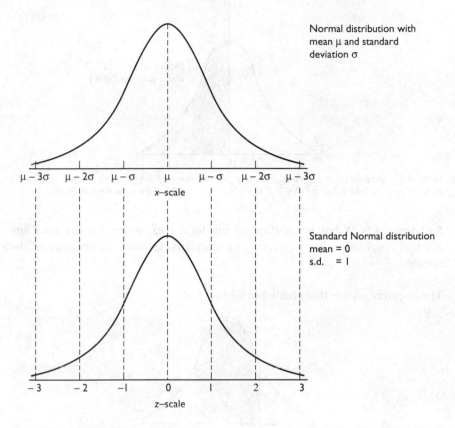

Normal distribution with mean μ and standard deviation σ

μ − 3σ   μ − 2σ   μ − σ   μ   μ − σ   μ − 2σ   μ − 3σ

x−scale

Standard Normal distribution
mean = 0
s.d.   = 1

− 3   − 2   −1   0   1   2   3

z−scale

Figure 4.34   Relationship between the probability density function curves of X ~ N(μ, σ²) and Z ~ N(0, 1)

The area under the probability distribution function curve of the standard Normal variate Z, from $Z = -\infty$ to $Z = z$, is conventionally abbreviated to $\Phi(z)$. In other words,

$$\Phi(z) = P(Z < z)$$

To determine this area for any z, Table I in the Appendix of Statistical Tables is used. Table I gives the area between $Z = 0$ and $Z = z$. However, since the curve is symmetrical about the mean ($z = 0$), it follows that:

$$P(Z < 0) = \Phi(0) = 0.5$$

Therefore $\Phi(z)$ can be obtained simply by adding 0.5 to the value found in Table I (see Figure 4.35). (Readers with a knowledge of calculus will recognize that $\Phi(z)$ is the definite integral, between the limits $-\infty$ and z, of the right-hand side of Equation 4.20. However, this expression cannot readily be integrated, and therefore it is more convenient to use Table I.)

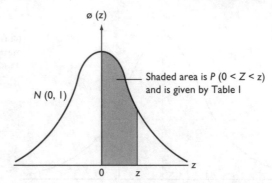

Figure 4.35 Area under the probability density function curve of the standard Normal distribution, N(0, 1), given by Table I. This is P(0 < Z < z). For P(Z < z) add 0.5 to the value given in Table I

Example 4.9   What proportion of the total area under the curve of any Normal distribution lies between one standard deviation either side of the mean?

The required area is that shaded in Figure 4.36.

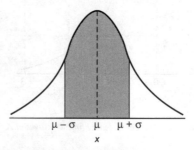

Figure 4.36 $P(\mu - \sigma < X < \mu + \sigma)$ where $X \sim N(\mu, \sigma^2)$

This area is equal to the shaded area under the standard Normal distribution shown in Figure 4.37.

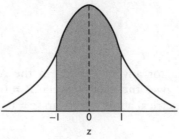

Figure 4.37 $P(-1 < Z < 1)$ where $Z \sim N(0, 1)$

Since the curve is symmetrical, the required area is twice the area shown in Figure 4.38.

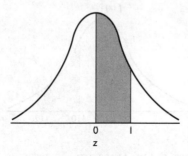

Figure 4.38   P(0 < Z <1) where Z ~ N(0, 1)

This area can now simply be looked up in Table I, under $z = 1.00$, as shown in Figure 4.39.

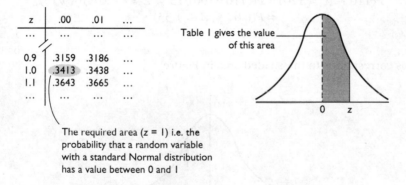

z	.00	.01	...
...	...	...	...
0.9	.3159	.3186	...
1.0	.3413	.3438	...
1.1	.3643	.3665	...
...	...	...	...

Table I gives the value of this area

The required area (z = 1) i.e. the probability that a random variable with a standard Normal distribution has a value between 0 and 1

Figure 4.39   P(0 < Z <1), where Z ~ N(0, 1), in Table I

The required area is twice that found in Table I, that is:

$$2(0.3413) = 0.6826$$

So 68.26% of the total area lies in the given interval.

Example 4.10   An intelligence quotient (IQ) test which has a mean of 100 and a standard deviation of 15 is administered. What percentage of the population would be expected to have an IQ score of between 110 and 120 (inclusive)?

Let X be the IQ of a randomly chosen member of the population. Then:

$$X \sim N(100, 15^2)$$

The required proportion is represented by the area shaded in Figure 4.40.

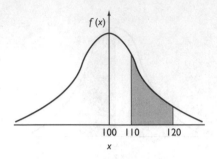

Figure 4.40   P($110 \leqslant X \leqslant 120$) *where* X ~ N($100, 15^2$).

Converting to the standard Normal variate Z using Equation 4.19:

$$P(110 \leqslant X \leqslant 120) = P((110-100)/15 \leqslant Z \leqslant (120-100)/15)$$
$$= P(0.67 \leqslant Z \leqslant 1.33)$$

This corresponds to the shaded area in Figure 4.41.

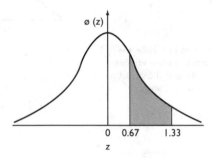

Figure 4.41   P($0.67 \leqslant Z \leqslant 1.33$) *where* Z ~ N($0, 1$)

Therefore the required area is given by:

$$\Phi(1.33) - \Phi(0.67)$$

From Table I, $\Phi(1.33) = 0.4082 + 0.5$, and $\Phi(0.67) = 0.2486 + 0.5$. Therefore the required proportion is:

$$0.4082 - 0.2486 = 0.1596$$

So the answer is 16.0%.

Two-tailed percentage points

The two-tailed 5 percentage points are the values of the Normal variate that divide the distribution into two tails (the shaded areas in Figure 4.42), each of which contains 2.5% of the total area. Together, these two tails contain 5% of the total area.

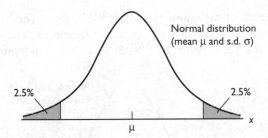

Figure 4.42   X ~ N(μ, σ^2); two-tailed 5 percentage points

Converting Figure 4.42 to the standard Normal distribution, the value of z that needs to be looked up in Table I is that shown in Figure 4.43.

Figure 4.43   Z ~ N(0, 1); two-tailed 5 percentage points

So, we need to look up 47.5%, that is 0.4750, in Table I and find the value of z corresponding to it (Figure 4.44).

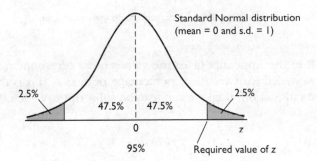

z	.00	...	.06	...
...	...	...	...	...
1.9	.4713	...	.4750	...
2.0	.4772	...	...	...

Figure 4.44   Part of Table I allowing the value of z to be looked up that corresponds to $\Phi(z) = (0.4750 + 0.5)$

So the required value of z is 1.96. Converting back to x, using Equation 4.19, we have:

$$x = \mu + 1.96\sigma \qquad (4.21)$$

Since the Normal distribution is symmetrical about the mean, this means that for any Normally distributed random variable the two-tailed 5% points are given by $(\mu + 1.96\sigma)$ and $(\mu - 1.96\sigma)$, as shown in Figure 4.45.

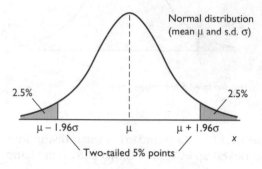

Statistics 4.45 s/s

Figure 4.45 X ~ N(μ, σ^2); two-tailed 5 percentage points in terms of μ and σ

Table II in the Appendix gives the values of z corresponding to commonly used two-tailed (or two-sided) percentage points, α. If α is the total area of the two tails cut off, then we can use the subscript $\alpha/2$ such that:

$$\Phi(z_{\alpha/2}) = P(Z < z_{\alpha/2}) = \alpha/2$$

So, in general, the two values of z that are the two-tailed 100α percentage points of $N(0, 1)$ are given by $z_{\alpha/2}$ and $z_{1-\alpha/2}$ as shown in Figure 4.46.

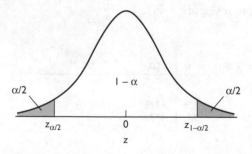

Figure 4.46 Z ~ N(0, 1); two-tailed 100α percentage points. Redrawn from Puri and Tyrer (1992) Sciences Basic to Psychiatry, with permission from Churchill Livingstone, Edinburgh, UK.

One-tailed percentage points

For $Z \sim N(0, 1)$ the one-tailed α percentage point is the value of z for which:

$$P(Z \geqslant z) = \alpha$$

This value is $z_{1-\alpha}$, as shown in Figure 4.47, which, since the curve is symmetrical, also equals $-z_\alpha$.

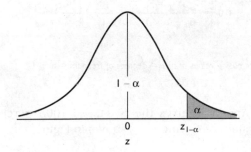

Figure 4.47 $Z \sim N(0, 1)$; one-tailed 100α percentage point

Table III in the Appendix gives the values of z corresponding to commonly used one-tailed (or one-sided) percentage points, α.

t DISTRIBUTION

Like the Normal distribution, the t distribution is a continuous probability distribution that is symmetrical about the mean. It has longer tails than the Normal distribution. In the next chapter we shall see that the t distribution is used in making inferences about the mean of a Normal population when its variance is unknown; in practice it is used when the sample size (n) is small ($n < 30$).

The sample size, n, defines the number of degrees of freedom, which for the t distribution is denoted by the Greek letter nu, ν, as follows

$$\nu = n - 1 \tag{4.22}$$

A t distribution with ν degrees of freedom can be written as $t(\nu)$ or as $t(n-1)$. Figure 4.48 shows the t distribution for increasing values of ν. As ν increases, $t(\nu)$ approaches the Normal distribution. In practice:

For $n \geqslant 30$, $t(\nu) \approx N(0, 1)$

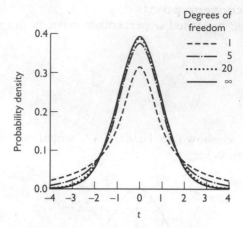

Figure 4.48   t(ν) for increasing values of n; ν = degrees of freedom = n − 1

Table IV in the Appendix gives the two-tailed 100α percentage points of $t(\nu)$, that is, the values of $t_{\alpha/2}$ and $t_{1-\alpha/2}$ shown in Figure 4.49.

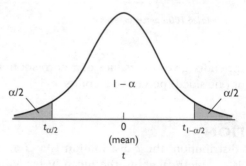

Figure 4.49   t(ν); two-tailed 100α percentage points. Redrawn from Puri and Tyrer (1992) Sciences Basic to Psychiatry, with permission from Churchill Livingstone, Edinburgh, UK.

χ^2 DISTRIBUTION

If W is the sum of the squares of ν independent variables, $_1$ to Z_ν, where each $Z \sim N(0, 1)$, then W follows the chi-squared distribution with ν degrees of freedom, written as $\chi^2(\nu)$. That is, if

$$W = \sum Z_i^2 \qquad \text{where } i = 1 \text{ to } \nu, \text{ and } Z_i \sim N(0, 1)$$

Then

$$W \sim \chi^2(\nu)$$

(Note that the Greek letter chi is pronounced with a hard ch, as in the word 'loch'.)

Unlike the Normal and t distributions, the chi-squared distribution is asymmetrical. For this reason, only the right-hand, one-tailed 100α percentage points are given for $\chi^2(\nu)$ in Table V in the Appendix, corresponding to Figure 4.50. The shape of the probability density function curve in Figure 4.50 varies with the value of ν.

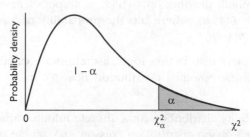

Figure 4.50 $\chi^2(\nu)$; *one-tailed 100α percentage point.* Redrawn from Puri and Tyrer (1992) *Sciences Basic to Psychiatry*, with permission from Churchill Livingstone, Edinburgh, UK.

F DISTRIBUTION

The F distribution is related to the χ^2 distribution and is likewise asymmetrical. A given F distribution is described in terms of ν_1 and ν_2, each of which gives a number of degrees of freedom. This is usually abbreviated to $F(\nu_1, \nu_2)$. The use of this distribution is described in Chapter 8.

SUMMARY

▨ If E can occur in n different ways out of a total of N likely possible ways, then $P(E) = n/N; 0 \leqslant P(E) \leqslant 1$.

▨ A probability of 0 implies that an event never occurs.

▨ A probability of 1 implies that an event always occurs.

▨ The sum of the probabilities that an event will occur and that it will not occur is equal to 1: $P(E) + P(\bar{E}) = 1$.

▨ $P(E_1$ or E_2 or $\ldots E_n) = P(E_1) + P(E_2) + \ldots + P(E_n)$, where $E_1, E_2, \ldots, E_n$ are mutually exclusive.

▨ $P(E_1$ and E_2 and $\ldots E_n) = P(E_1)P(E_2) \ldots P(E_n)$, where $E_1, E_2, \ldots, E_n$ are independent.

▨ When a trial or experiment is repeated a large number of times, in the long run the relative frequency of a given event approaches the probability of that event occurring.

▨ The number of ways r objects can be chosen from n, paying attention to the order in which they are chosen, is given by $^nP_r = n!/(n-r)!$

▨ The number of ways r objects can be chosen from n, regardless of order, is given by $^nC_r = n!/[\, r!(n-r)!\,]$.

▓ $0! = 1$.

▓ The sum of all the probabilities in a discrete probability distribution is 1; the area under the probability density function curve of a continuous probability distribution is 1.

▓ The probability distribution for a discrete binary variable (range = 0, 1) is the Bernoulli distribution, which is a special case of the binomial distribution $B(1, p)$, where p is the probability of 'success'; mean = p, variance = $p(1-p)$.

▓ The probability distribution for a discrete finite variable (range = 0, 1, 2, ..., n) is the binomial distribution $B(n, p)$; mean = np, variance = $np(1-p)$.

▓ The probability distribution for a discrete infinite variable (range = 0, 1, 2, ...) is the Poisson distribution Poisson: (μ), where $\mu = np$; mean = μ, variance = μ.

▓ The probability distribution for a continuous variable (range = $\mathbb{R}$, the real number line) is the Normal distribution $N(\mu, \sigma^2)$; mean = μ, variance = σ^2.

▓ If $X \sim N(\mu, \sigma^2)$, then the standard Normal variate Z is obtained from $Z = (X - \mu)/\sigma$.

▓ For $Z \sim N(0, 1)$, mean = 0, variance = 1; cumulative distribution function, $P(Z < z)$, is given by $\Phi(z)$.

▓ For $N(\mu, \sigma^2)$ the two-tailed 5% points are given by $\mu \pm 1.96\sigma$.

▓ When $n < 30$, the t distribution $t(\nu)$ is used in making inferences about the mean of a Normal population when its variance is unknown (the number of degrees of freedom, $\nu = n-1$); for $n \geqslant 30$, $t(\nu) \approx N(0, 1)$.

▓ The chi-squared distribution with ν degrees of freedom, $\chi^2(\nu)$, and the related F distribution are asymmetrical continuous probability distributions.

EXERCISE

1   A card is randomly chosen from a deck of 52 playing cards.

(a) What is the probability that it will be a heart?
(b) What is the probability that it will not be a heart?

2   What is the probability that one throw of a die will result in a 1, 2 or 4?

3   1000 trials of an experiment are carried out. In each trial 3 dice are thrown together. How many times, on average, would you expect to throw three sixes together in the 1000 trials?

4   Calculate 10!

5   In how many ways can 5 objects be chosen from 10, paying attention to the order in which they are chosen?

6   In how many ways can 5 objects be chosen from 10, regardless of order?

7   What is the probability that in 6 throws of a die the number of 'sixes' thrown is 2?

8   What is the standard deviation of a Poisson distribution with mean 4?

9   What are the effects on a Normal distribution of:
(a) an increase in the mean
(b) a decrease in the standard deviation?

10   A random variable follows a Normal distribution with mean 75 and standard deviation 4. What is the probability that the random variable has a value between 76.1 and 77.0 (inclusive)?

11   Which of the following probability distributions are symmetrical?

(a) $t(3)$ (e) $N(75, 16)$
(b) $N(0, 1)$ (f) $B(8, 1/3)$
(c) $\chi^2(10)$ (g) Poisson (2)
(d) $F(4, 24)$ (h) $B(6, 1/2)$

CHAPTER 5

From samples to populations: estimation and hypothesis testing

SAMPLING

In Chapter 1 we looked at the differences between samples and populations. We saw that often it is not possible to obtain information about all members of a given finite population; for example, it is not possible to make all the measurements in an infinite population. Hence there is a need for sampling (Figure 5.1).

METHODS OF SAMPLING

A *simple random sample* is a sample chosen from a given population such that every possible sample of the same size has the same probability of being chosen. In order to save time and effort, a *systematic* type of sampling can be used instead. A few common examples are described here. Other methods are beyond the scope of this book.

Periodic sampling

In this type of sampling every *n*th member of the population is chosen. For example, in Figure 5.2 every third patient attending an outpatient department has been chosen. However, this may not always lead to a random choice owing to some unforeseen underlying pattern.

Using random numbers

Using random numbers can be a better method than periodic sampling for ensuring random choice. The random numbers can be obtained from a computer program (e.g. RND returns a single-precision random number between 0 and 1 in QBasic), a scientific calculator with a (pseudo)random number generator (labelled RAN# on many calculators), or a table of random numbers. Figure 5.3 gives an example of one way to use a list of random numbers to choose every fifth patient.

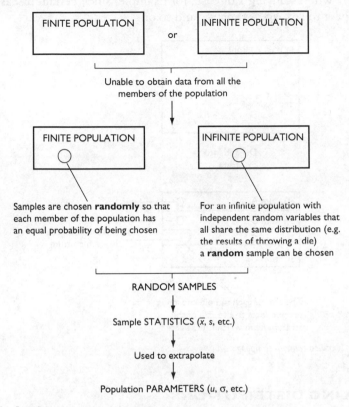

Figure 5.1 *Sampling*

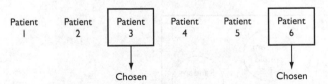

Figure 5.2 *Periodic sampling: every third patient attending outpatients has been chosen*

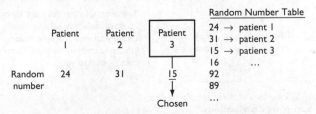

Figure 5.3 *Random sampling using random numbers: in this example each patient is assigned a random number and those with a random number ending with 0 or 5 are chosen*

Stratified random sampling

In this method a given population is stratified before random samples are chosen from each stratum, as shown in Figure 5.4. This is a useful method to employ when studying a disease, for example, since certain diseases vary with respect to sex, age, ethnicity, and so on.

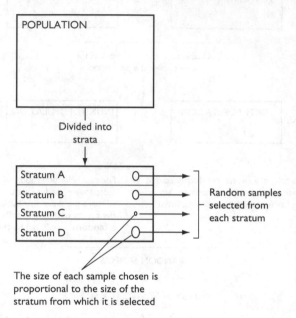

Figure 5.4   Stratified random sampling

SAMPLING DISTRIBUTIONS

In Figure 5.5, three random samples, A to C, have been chosen from a given population. The sample statistics (e.g. sample means and sample standard

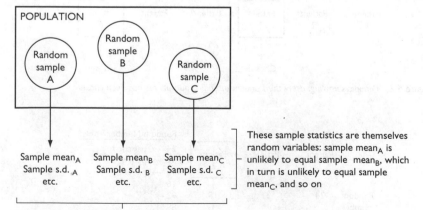

Figure 5.5   Sampling distributions (s.d. = standard deviation)

deviations) from A to C are themselves random variables. It is unlikely that $\bar{x}_A = \bar{x}_B = \bar{x}_C$, that $s_A = s_B = s_C$, and so on. The probability distributions of these sample statistics are sampling distributions. The mean and standard deviation of sampling distributions are now given without proof.

Mean of the sampling distribution of $\bar{x}$

For a parent population with mean μ, the sample mean, $\bar{x}$, gives an unbiased estimate of μ. That is:

$$\text{Mean of the sampling distribution of } \bar{x} = \mu \qquad (5.1)$$

Standard error of the mean

The standard error of the mean is another name for the standard deviation of the sampling distribution of $\bar{x}$. For a parent population of size n, with standard deviation σ:

$$\text{Standard error of the mean} = \sigma/\sqrt{n} \qquad (5.2)$$

From Equation 5.2 it is clear that the standard deviation of $\bar{x}$ decreases as n increases. In other words, the larger the sample size, the more confident we can be that $\bar{x}$ is close to the population mean μ.

Other standard errors

Other standard errors (standard deviations of sampling distributions) are now stated.

Consider two independent samples (taken from the same parent population) of sizes n_1 and n_2, and respective standard deviations s_1 and s_2, where s_1 and s_2 have similar values, and means $\bar{x}_1$ and $\bar{x}_2$. It can be shown that the:

$$\text{Standard error of the difference between } \bar{x}_1 \text{ and } \bar{x}_2 = s\sqrt{\frac{1}{n_1} + \frac{1}{n_2}}$$

$$(5.3)$$

where the pooled standard deviation s is given by:

$$s = \sqrt{\frac{(n_1 - 1)s_1^2 + (n_2 - 1)s_2^2}{n_1 + n_2 - 2}} \qquad (5.4)$$

and the number of degrees of freedom is $n_1 + n_2 - 2$.

If $n_1 = n_2$, then Equation 5.4 simplifies to:

$$s = \sqrt{\frac{s_1^2 + s_2^2}{2}} \qquad (5.5)$$

The mean of the sampling distribution of a sample proportion is equal to the true population proportion, p. For a random sample of size n, the standard deviation of the sampling distribution is given by:

$$\text{Standard error of the proportion } (p) = \sqrt{\frac{p(1 - p)}{n}} \qquad (5.6)$$

For two independent samples of sizes n_1 and n_2, and respective observed proportions p_1 and p_2:

$$\begin{array}{l}\text{Standard error of the difference between} \\ \text{sample proportions } (p_1 \text{ and } p_2)\end{array} = \sqrt{\frac{p_1(1 - p_1)}{n_1} + \frac{p_2(1 - p_2)}{n_2}} \qquad (5.7)$$

THE CENTRAL LIMIT THEOREM

When the parent population is Normal, $N(\mu, \sigma^2)$, then the sampling distribution of the mean of random samples from it, $\bar{X}$, will also be Normal, with mean μ and standard deviation $\sigma/\sqrt{n}$ (see Equations 5.1 and 5.2). That is, $\bar{X} \sim N(\mu, \sigma^2/n)$.

The central limit theorem (which is not proved in this book) tells us that even if the parent population (with mean μ and finite standard deviation σ) is *not* Normal, so long as the sample size n is large enough ($n \geqslant 30$), then the sampling distribution of the mean of random samples from it, $\bar{X}$, will be approximately Normal, with mean μ and standard deviation $\sigma/\sqrt{n}$. That is:

$$\text{For } n \geqslant 30 \text{ and } \sigma \neq \infty, \qquad \bar{X} \approx N(\mu, \sigma^2/n) \qquad (5.8)$$

As n increases, the distribution of $\bar{X}$ approaches $N(\mu, \sigma^2/n)$.

Standardizing Equation 5.8, we have:

$$\text{For } n \geqslant 30 \text{ and } \sigma \neq \infty, \qquad \frac{\bar{X} - \mu}{\sigma/\sqrt{n}} \approx N(0,1) \qquad (5.9)$$

This is a powerful result, as it allows properties of the Normal distribution to be applied to samples from non-Normal parent populations.

SPSS for Windows

From the above discussion it is clear that when the sample size is less than 30 it may be important to test whether the sample data come from a Normal distribution. With SPSS a Normal probability plot can be derived from the data. In this graph the cumulative distribution of the observed variable is plotted on the horizontal axis and the cumulative distribution expected from the Normal distribution is plotted against it on the vertical axis. The closer the sample is from a Normal distribution, the nearer the Normal probability plot is to a straight line with a positive gradient. A detrended Normal probability plot shows the deviations of the plotted points from a straight line; for a Normally distributed variable no pattern should be seen. SPSS automatically plots both types of graph at the same time.

Select Graphics
      Normal P-P
            OK

SPSS also allows numerical statistical tests of Normality to be computed (the Kolmogorov–Smirnov test).

Select Statistics
      Nonparametric tests
            1-Sample K-S...
            OK

ESTIMATION: CONFIDENCE INTERVALS

From sample statistics, confidence statements can be made about the corresponding unknown population parameters, by constructing confidence intervals. A confidence interval can be two-sided or one-sided; unless otherwise stated, confidence intervals calculated in this book are two-sided and symmetrical (central).

If a $100(1-\alpha)\%$ confidence interval from a statistic (or statistics) is calculated, this implies that if the study were repeated with other random samples taken from the same parent population and further $100(1-\alpha)\%$ confidence intervals similarly individually calculated, the overall proportion of these confidence intervals which included the corresponding population parameter(s) would tend to $100(1-\alpha)\%$.

A commonly used value of α is 0.05, corresponding to a 95% confidence interval.

CONFIDENCE INTERVAL FOR μ: $n \geqslant 30$

We shall first consider how to calculate a confidence interval for the population mean, μ, when the sample size is large, that is, $n \geqslant 30$. Under these conditions, the central limit theorem applies (see Equation 5.8). From the last chapter we know that the two-tailed 100α percentage points are $z_{\alpha/2}$ and $z_{1-\alpha/2}$. So these two values of z bound an area that is $(1-\alpha)$, that is, $100(1-\alpha)\%$ of the total area under the probability density function curve of the standard Normal distribution (see Figures. 4.46 and 5.6).

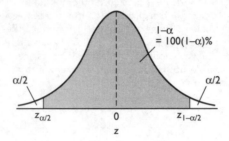

Figure 5.6　$Z \sim N(0, 1)$; area bounded by $z_{\alpha/2}$ and $z_{1-\alpha/2}$

By substituting the two two-tailed 100α percentage points into Equation 5.9 we obtain the $100(1-\alpha)\%$ confidence interval for μ:

$$\bar{x} + z_{\alpha/2}\frac{\sigma}{\sqrt{n}} < \mu < \bar{x} + z_{1-\alpha/2}\frac{\sigma}{\sqrt{n}} \tag{5.10}$$

So, using two-tailed 100α percentage points from Table II, we can see that the 95% confidence interval is given by:

$$\bar{x} - 1.96\sigma/\sqrt{n} < \mu < \bar{x} + 1.96\sigma/\sqrt{n} \tag{5.11}$$

Similarly, the 99% confidence interval is:

$$\bar{x} - 2.58\sigma/\sqrt{n} < \mu < \bar{x} + 2.58\sigma/\sqrt{n} \tag{5.12}$$

Example 5.1 The mortality experiences of a hospitalized mentally handicapped population between 1981 and 1990 (inclusive) were examined by Puri *et al.* (1995a). During these 10 years there was a total of 325 deaths in the hospital studied. The overall mean age of death was 68.4 years (standard deviation 18.2 years). Calculate a 95% confidence interval for the true mean age of death during those years for similarly hospitalized mentally handicapped patients.

Using conventional notation and omitting units, we have:

Sample mean, $\bar{x} = 68.4$
Sample standard deviation, $s = 18.2$
Sample size, $n = 325$

Using s as an estimate of σ, since $n \geqslant 30$ we can substitute in Equation 5.11 to obtain the 95% confidence interval of μ:

$68.4 - 1.96(18.2/\sqrt{(325)}) < \mu < 68.4 + 1.96(18.2/\sqrt{(325)})$
$\therefore \ 66.4 < \mu < 70.4$ (to 1 decimal place)

So the required confidence interval is 66.4 to 70.4 years.

CONFIDENCE INTERVAL FOR μ: $n < 30$

When the sample size is too small to allow the central limit theorem to be applied, then a confidence interval for the population mean can be calculated using the t distribution, so long as it is valid to assume that the population is Normal or approximately so. Using standard notation, as indicated in Figure 4.49, the required confidence interval is:

$$\bar{x} + t_{\alpha/2}\frac{s}{\sqrt{n}} < \mu < \bar{x} + t_{1-\alpha/2}\frac{s}{\sqrt{n}} \qquad (5.13)$$

Example 5.2 In a study of firesetters by Puri *et al.* (1995b) it was found that the mean age of a sample of 22 male firesetters was 27.2 years (standard deviation 13.0 years). Calculate the corresponding 95% confidence interval for the true population mean age.

Using conventional notation and omitting units, we have:

Sample mean, $\bar{x} = 27.2$
Sample standard deviation, $s = 13.0$
Sample size, $n = 22$
$\therefore$ Degrees of freedom, $\nu = n - 1 = 21$

From Table IV the two-tailed 100α percentage points for $\alpha = 0.05$ are ± 2.080.

Substituting in Equation 5.13, the 95% confidence interval of μ is given by:

$$27.2 - 2.080(13.0/\sqrt{22}) < \mu < 27.2 + 2.080(13.0/\sqrt{22})$$
$$\therefore \quad 21.4 < \mu < 33.0 \quad \text{(to 1 decimal place)}$$

So the required confidence interval is 21.4 to 33.0 years.

OTHER CONFIDENCE INTERVALS

In general, the $100(1-\alpha)$% confidence interval for a population parameter is given by:

$$\begin{aligned}&[\text{statistic} + t_{\alpha/2}(\text{standard error})] \text{ to} \\ &[\text{statistic} + t_{1-\alpha/2}(\text{standard error})]\end{aligned} \qquad (5.14)$$

When it is appropriate to use the Normal distribution (for example when $n \geq 30$, or when dealing with proportions (for which n is not important)), the $100(1-\alpha)$% confidence interval for the population parameter is given by:

$$\begin{aligned}&[\text{statistic} + z_{\alpha/2}(\text{standard error})] \text{ to} \\ &[\text{statistic} + z_{1-\alpha/2}(\text{standard error})]\end{aligned} \qquad (5.15)$$

Example 5.3   In the study of firesetters by Puri *et al.* (1995b) mentioned in Example 5.2, it was also found that the mean age of a sample of 8 female firesetters was 24.2 years (standard deviation 7.2 years). Calculate the corresponding 95% confidence interval for the difference in the population mean ages of male and female firesetters.

Denoting males with the suffix 1 and females with the suffix 2, and omitting units, we have:

$$\begin{aligned}&\bar{x}_1 = 27.2 \qquad\quad \bar{x}_2 = 24.2 \\ &s_1 = 13.0 \qquad\quad s_2 = 7.2 \\ &n_1 = 22 \qquad\quad\; n_2 = 8\end{aligned}$$
$\therefore$ Difference between the two sample means $= \bar{x}_1 - \bar{x}_2 = 3$

Substituting in Equation 5.4, the pooled standard deviation, s, is given by:

$$\begin{aligned}s &= \sqrt{\{[(22-1)(13.0)^2 + (8-1)(7.2)^2]/[22 + 8 - 2]\}} \\ &= 11.82\end{aligned}$$

From Equation 5.3, the standard error of the difference between the two sample means is:

$11.82\sqrt{[(1/22) + (1/8)]} = 4.88$

Degrees of freedom $= n_1 + n_2 - 2 = 28$

From Table IV the two-tailed 100α percentage points for $\alpha = 0.05$ are ± 2.048. Substituting in Equation 5.14, the required confidence interval is:

$3 - 2.048(4.88)$ to $3 + 2.048(4.88) = -7.0$ to 13.0 (to 1 decimal place)

So the required confidence interval is -7.0 to 13.0 years.

(Since this confidence interval includes the value zero, we can conclude that at the 5% significance level ($\alpha = 0.05$) the difference in the mean ages of the males and females is not statistically significant. Statistical significance is considered in the next section.)

SPSS for Windows

Confidence interval for mean
Select Statistics
    Summarize
        Explore
        Statistics
        Enter confidence interval for mean if not the default 95%
        OK

Confidence interval for difference between means
Select Statistics
    Compare Means
        Independent-Samples T Test (or another option if more appropriate)
        Enter Test Variable(s) and Grouping Variable (e.g. in Example 5.3 AGE would be the Test Variable and SEX the Grouping Variable)
        (If confidence interval $\neq$ 95% (default), click on Options and enter new confidence interval $\rightarrow$ Continue)
        OK

The program automatically checks if the variances of the two groups are significantly different, using Levene's Test for Equality of Variances. An example of part of the output from SPSS is shown in Figure 5.7. If they are *not* significantly different (using the *F* distribution) the value of the probability adjacent to the value of *F* is greater than α, as is the case in Figure 5.7:

$$F = .000 \qquad P = .985$$

In this case the appropriate results are those in the row labelling the variances Equal (see Figure 5.7). Conversely, if the variances are to be taken as unequal (*F* has a value corresponding to a probability $< \alpha$), take the results from the Unequal row.

Levene's Test for Equality of Variances: F=.000 P=.985

Variances	t-value	df	2-Tail Sig	SE of Diff	95% CI for Diff
Equal	−2.21	70	.030	2.747	(−11.548, −.590)
Unequal	−2.15	50.61	.036	2.817	(−11.726, −.413)

t-test for Equality of Means

Figure 5.7   *Part of the output from SPSS when comparing two means*

HYPOTHESIS TESTING

In the previous section on estimation we saw how, having carried out a study, we can use the sample statistic(s) from that study to estimate a confidence interval for corresponding unknown population parameter(s). In this section the approach is as follows: the value (or range of values) of the unknown population parameter is first hypothesized, and this hypothesis is then tested by carrying out the study and determining whether or not the sample statistic(s) imply that the hypothesis should be rejected. The approach is thus one of hypothesis testing rather than estimation.

TYPES OF HYPOTHESIS

The initial hypothesis concerning the value of the unknown population parameter is the *null hypothesis*, conventionally written as H_0. Suppose we wish to discover whether a new treatment A is more effective than an existing treatment B. The simplest hypothesis to test would be that there is *no difference* in effectiveness between A and B. H_0 usually postulates the state of no difference. (We may formulate H_0 simply in order to try to reject it.)

When H_0 is formulated, an *alternative hypothesis*, H_1, is also formulated. H_1 disagrees with H_0 and is accepted only if H_0 is rejected.

A *simple hypothesis* entails one hypothesized value for the population parameter. For example, the hypothesized null hypothesis might be that the population mean equals 34 units, that is, $H_0 : \mu = 34$.

A *composite hypothesis* is one that entails more than one hypothesized value for the population parameter. For example, the hypothesized alternative hypothesis might be that the population mean does not equal 34 units, that is, $H_1 : \mu \neq 34$. If a composite alternative hypothesis were of the form $H_1 : \mu > 34$ (or $H_1 : \mu < 34$), then it would also be *one-sided*; a composite alternative hypothesis of the type $H_1 : \mu \neq 34$ is known as *two-sided*.

In general, two-sided tests of significance should be used; a one-sided test should be used if a large difference in one direction would lead to the same action as no difference at all, and in this case the direction of the test should be specified in advance. Importantly, expectation of a difference in a particular direction is not an adequate justification for using a one-sided test (Bland and Altman, 1994).

TYPES OF ERROR
There are clearly two types of error that could occur in hypothesis testing, shown in Table 5.1.

A *type I error* is the error of wrongly rejecting H_0 when it is true. The probability of making a type I error is denoted by α.

A *type II error* is the error of wrongly accepting H_0 when it is false. The probability of making a type II error is denoted by β.

SIGNIFICANCE LEVEL
The level of significance is defined as the probability of making a type I error, and therefore is equal to α.

POWER
The power of a hypothesis test is the probability that H_0 is rejected when it is indeed false. From Table 5.1 it is evident that it is equal to $1-\beta$.

Table 5.1 Hypothesis testing: types of error and their probabilities

	H_0 accepted	H_0 rejected	Total probability
H_0 true	Decision correct Probability = $1-\alpha$	Type I error Probability = α = significance level	1
H_0 false	Type II error Probability = β	Decision correct Probability = $1-\beta$ = power	1

METHOD

Hypothesis testing is carried out as follows. Formulate H_0 and H_1, and specify the significance level, α. Select the test statistic, which is calculated from:

Test statistic = (appropriate statistic − hypothesized
parameter)/(standard error of statistic)   (5.16)

From the sampling distribution of the test statistic create the test criterion for testing H_0 *versus* H_1. Carry out the study/experiment and calculate the value of the test statistic from the sample data. Calculate the difference, d, between the value of the test statistic from the sample and that expected from H_0. The value of the test statistic expected from H_0 (the one- or two-tailed 100α percentage points) are the *critical value(s)* of the test statistic (see Figure 5.8). Calculate $P(d)$.

- If $P(d) < \alpha$, the result is *statistically significant* at the level of α (that is, d is considered too great to be attributed to chance), and H_0 is rejected.

- If $P(d) \geqslant \alpha$, the result is not statistically significant at the level of α (that is, d may be attributed to chance), and H_0 cannot be rejected. H_0 is then either accepted or judgement is reserved; reserving judgement is a way of avoiding a type II error.

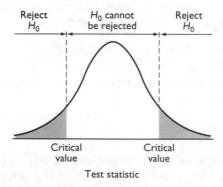

Figure 5.8   A two-tailed test

The application of this method is demonstrated in the following examples. Note that as α is reduced, the probability of a type I error diminishes but the probability of a type II error increases. In practice, α is usually chosen as 0.05 (5%) or 0.01 (1%).

Example 5.4   Returning to the study of firesetters by Puri *et al.* (1995b) mentioned in Examples 5.2 and 5.3, use the above method to test the null hypothesis, at the 5% level of significance, that there is no difference between the population mean ages of male and female firesetters.

(In Example 5.3 we have already calculated that the 95% confidence interval for the difference between the population means includes zero, but this result is ignored for the purpose of this Example.)

Using the same nomenclature as in Example 5.3, and omitting units, we have:

$H_0 : \mu_1 = \mu_2$
$H_1 : \mu_1 \neq \mu_2$ (two-sided)
$\alpha = 0.05$
Degrees of freedom $= n_1 + n_2 - 2 = 28$
Appropriate statistic $= \bar{x}_1 - \bar{x}_2 = 3$
Hypothesized parameter $= \mu_1 - \mu_2 = 0$ (since $H_0 : \mu_1 = \mu_2$)

The standard error of $(\bar{x}_1 - \bar{x}_2)$ is given by Equations 5.3 and 5.4 and, from Example 5.3, equals 4.88. So, substituting in Equation 5.16, and using the t distribution, the test statistic is given by:

$$t = 3/4.88 = 0.61$$

From Table IV, for $\alpha = 0.05$ the critical values (two-tailed) are given by $t(28) = \pm 2.048$. Since $-2.048 < 0.61 < 2.048$, we cannot reject H_0 (see Figure 5.9).

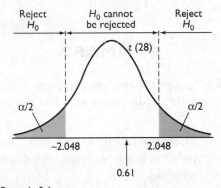

Figure 5.9   Testing H_0 in Example 5.4

(In theory, before using the t test in the way we have just done, we should check that the variances of the two groups are not significantly different at the 5% level using the F distribution. In practice, however, this step is automatically carried out by most computer programs, such as SPSS, and even if the two variances are significantly different, the program will give adjusted probabilities corresponding to the value of t.)

SPSS for Windows

The steps are essentially the same as those given in the previous section. For example, to test whether two means are significantly different:

Select Statistics
    Compare Means
        Independent-Samples T Test (or another option if more appropriate)
        Enter Test Variable(s) and Grouping Variable (e.g. in Example 5.3 AGE
        would be the Test Variable and SEX the Grouping Variable)
        OK

The program automatically checks if the variances of the two groups are significantly different, using Levene's Test for Equality of Variances (see Figure 5.7). If they are *not* significantly different (using the F distribution) the value of the probability adjacent to the value of F is greater than α, as is the case in Figure 5.7:

    $F = .000 \quad P = .985$

In this case the two-tailed significance probability to read off is that in the row labelling the variances Equal (.030 in Figure 5.7). Conversely, if the variances are to be taken as unequal (F has a value corresponding to a probability $< \alpha$), take the results from the Unequal row. If the probability given (e.g. 0.030 in Figure 5.7) is less than α, then H_0 is rejected (the result is 'statistically significant'). If the probability is greater than α, H_0 cannot be rejected (the result is 'not statistically significant').

SUMMARY

- A simple random sample is one chosen from a population such that every possible sample of the same size has the same probability of being chosen.

- Systematic types of sampling include periodic sampling (every nth member of the population is chosen), the use of random numbers, and stratified random sampling.

- The probability distributions of sample statistics are sampling distributions.

- The mean of the sampling distribution of $\bar{x} = \mu$.

- The standard error of the mean (i.e. the standard deviation of the sampling distribution of $\bar{x}$) $= \sigma/\sqrt{n}$.

- If the parent population is Normal, $N(\mu, \sigma^2)$, then the sampling distribution of the mean of random samples from it, $\bar{X} \sim N(\mu, \sigma^2/n)$.

▪ From the central limit theorem, even if the parent population is not Normal, for $n \geqslant 30$, and $\sigma \neq \infty$, $\bar{X} \sim N(\mu, \sigma^2/n)$.

▪ A $100(1-\alpha)\%$ confidence interval calculated from a statistic implies that if the study were repeated with other random samples taken from the same population and further $100(1-\alpha)\%$ confidence intervals calculated, the overall proportion of these confidence intervals which included the corresponding parameter would tend to $100(1-\alpha)\%$.

▪ In estimation, having carried out a study, its sample statistic(s) are used to estimate a confidence interval for corresponding unknown population parameter(s).

▪ For $n \geqslant 30$, the confidence interval for μ is $\bar{x} + z_{\alpha/2}(\sigma/\sqrt{n}) < \mu < \bar{x} + z_{1-\alpha/2}(\sigma/\sqrt{n})$.

▪ For $n < 30$, if the population is (approximately) Normal, the confidence interval for μ is $\bar{x} + t_{\alpha/2}(s/\sqrt{n}) < \mu < \bar{x} + t_{1-\alpha/2}(s/\sqrt{n})$.

▪ In general, when it is appropriate to use the Normal distribution, the $100(1-\alpha)\%$ confidence interval for the population parameter is given by: [statistic + $z_{\alpha/2}$(standard error)] to [statistic + $z_{1-\alpha/2}$(standard error)].

▪ In hypothesis testing, the value (or range of values) of the unknown population parameter is first hypothesized, and this hypothesis is then tested by carrying out the study and determining whether or not the sample statistic(s) imply that the hypothesis should be rejected.

▪ The null hypothesis, H_0, is the initial hypothesis concerning the value of the unknown population parameter and disagrees with the alternative hypothesis, H_1.

▪ A type I error is the error of wrongly rejecting H_0 when it is true. The probability of making a type I error is α, the level of significance.

▪ A type II error is the error of wrongly accepting H_0 when it is false. The probability of making a type II error is denoted by β.

▪ The power of a hypothesis test is the probability that H_0 is rejected when it is indeed false. It is equal to $1-\beta$.

▪ In hypothesis testing the test statistic = (appropriate statistic − hypothesized parameter)/(standard error of statistic).

▪ The value of the test statistic expected from H_0 (the one- or two-tailed 100α percentage points) are the critical value(s) of the test statistic.

▪ If P(difference between the value of the test statistic from the sample and that expected from H_0) < α, the result is statistically significant at the level of α and H_0 is rejected.

▪ If P(difference between the value of the test statistic from the sample and that expected from H_0) $\geqslant \alpha$, the result is not statistically significant at the level of α and H_0 cannot be rejected. H_0 is then either accepted or judgement is reserved; reserving judgement is a way of avoiding a type II error.

EXERCISE

1 What is a simple random sample?

2 What is the difference between periodic sampling and stratified random sampling?

3 What is a sampling distribution?

4 State the mean and standard error (standard deviation) of the sampling distribution of the sample mean.

5 State the central limit theorem and explain its importance.

6 Compare and contrast estimation and hypothesis testing.

7 Define the following terms in relation to hypothesis testing:

   (a) type I error
   (b) type II error
   (c) power.

8 Following treatment with a trial drug, the plasma concentration of a certain substance is measured in 25 patients and found to have a mean value of 204 $\mu U \ l^{-1}$ (standard deviation 43.2 $\mu U \ l^{-1}$). Calculate a 95% confidence interval for the true mean.

9 In a study of the behavioural characteristics of patients suffering acute myocardial infarction, four and 12 months after random allocation to exercise training or light exercise, it was found that of 75 patients allocated to exercise training, 67 were working at 4 months (Worcester *et al.*, 1993). What percentage of patients allocated to exercise training were working at 4 months? Calculate the 95% confidence interval for the true percentage.

10 Bullock *et al.* (1990) reported that the mean age of 104 offenders on entering youth treatment centres was 15.2 (standard deviation 1.4) years. The mean age at the time of conviction for a group of 24 offenders detained in a young offenders' institution was more recently found to be 16.1 (standard deviation 0.6) years (Puri *et al.*, 1995c). Are the two mean ages significantly different? Give a 95% confidence interval for the true difference in mean ages.

REFERENCES

Bland, J. M. and Altman, D. G. (1994) One and two sided tests of significance. *BMJ*, **309**, 248.

Bullock, R., Hosie, K., Little, M. and Millham, S. (1990) The characteristics of young people in youth treatment centres: a study based on leavers from St Charles and Glenthorne between 1982 and 1985. *Journal of Forensic Psychiatry*, **1**, 329-50.

Puri, B. K., Lekh, S. K., Langa, A., Zaman, R. and Singh, I. (1995a) Mortality in a hospitalized mentally handicapped population: a ten year survey. *Journal of Intellectual Disability Research* (in press).

Puri, B. K., Baxter, R. and Cordess, C. C. (1995b) Characteristics of firesetters: a study and proposed multiaxial psychiatric classification. *British Journal of Psychiatry,* **166**, 393-6.

Puri, B. K., Lambert, M. T. and Cordess, C. C. (1995c) Characteristics of young offenders detained under Section 53(2) at a Young Offenders' Institution. *Medicine, Science and the Law* (in press).

Worcester, M. C., Hare, D. L., Oliver, R. G., Reid, M. A. and Goble, A. J. (1993) Early programmes of high and low intensity exercise and quality of life after acute myocardial infarction. *BMJ,* **307**, 1244-7.

CHAPTER 6

Contingency tables

In this chapter we shall see how to compare independent qualitative and discrete quantitative variables presented in the form of contingency tables.

The parent populations of the samples compared do not have to have any particular distribution (in particular, they do not have to be Normal). The χ^2 test and Fisher's exact test described in this chapter are examples of *non-parametric* (or distribution-free) tests. Other non-parametric tests are described in Chapter 9.

When the χ^2 and Fisher's exact tests are used to analyse contingency tables, the actual values of the data (the frequencies) must be employed in the tables; proportions (including percentages) must not be used.

χ^2 TEST: MORE THAN ONE DEGREE OF FREEDOM

Suppose we wished to determine whether a certain type of immunization is associated with the prevention of a given infection. The results for a random sample of 50 people might be as shown in Table 6.1. Such a table is a *contingency table* and is one type of problem to which the χ^2 test may be applied.

Another type of problem which the χ^2 test can be applied to is multinomial

Table 6.1 An example of a contingency table (see text)

	Protected	Not protected	Total
Immunized	9	31	40
Not immunized	2	8	10
Total	11	39	50

trials; that is, trials with more than two possible outcomes (rather than binomial trials).

CONTINGENCY TABLE

The core of a hypothetical 4×2 contingency table is shown in Figure 6.1. (Note that 4×2 is pronounced 'four by two'; that is, there are 4 rows and 2 columns.)

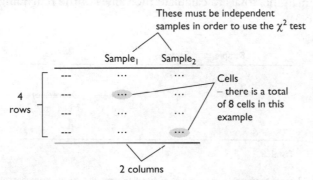

Figure 6.1 *The structure of a 4×2 contingency table.* Redrawn from Puri and Tyrer (1992) *Sciences Basic to Psychiatry*, with permission from Churchill Livingstone, Edinburgh, UK.

In order to use the χ^2 test the samples must be independent.

For the purposes of using the χ^2 distribution, the number of degrees of freedom, v, of a contingency table is given by:

$$v = (\text{number of rows}-1)(\text{number of columns}-1) \qquad (6.1)$$

Example 6.1 How many degrees of freedom does a 4×2 contingency table have?

From Equation 6.1:

$$\text{Degrees of freedom} = (4-1)(2-1) = 3$$

The contingency table shown in Figure 6.1 can be expanded by adding marginal totals for the rows and columns, as shown in Figure 6.2.

	Sample$_1$	Sample$_2$	Total
---	...	...	o o o
---	...	...	o o o
---	...	...	o o o
---	...	...	o o o
Total	o o o	o o o	...

Total of rows

Total of columns   Sum of cells

Figure 6.2 *A 4×2 contingency table with marginal totals added.* Redrawn from Puri and Tyrer (1992) *Sciences Basic to Psychiatry*, with permission from Churchill Livingstone, Edinburgh, UK.

The addition of a row and column of marginal totals does not alter the degrees of freedom. In general, marginal totals are not counted when applying Equation 6.1. Indeed, the degrees of freedom of a contingency table can be thought of as the minimum number of cells that need to be filled in order to allow the remaining cell values to be calculated by referring to the marginal totals. For instance, in the case of a 4 × 2 contingency table, if we have the values of any three independent cells, we can use the marginal totals to calculate the values of the remaining five cells (see Figure 6.3).

	Sample$_1$	Sample$_2$	Total	
---	√	?	√	
---	√	?	√	Degrees of
---	?	√	√	freedom = 3
---	?	?	√	
Total	√	√	√	

Figure 6.3 4 × 2 contingency table: the degrees of freedom gives the minimum number of independent cell values needed to calculate the remaining cell values from the marginal totals. From the values ticked, including the values of any three independent cells, the values of the remaining cells can be calculated by subtraction from the marginal totals. Three is the minimum number of cells for which this is true, i.e. the number of degrees of freedom is three. Redrawn from Puri and Tyrer (1992) Sciences Basic to Psychiatry, with permission from Churchill Livingstone, Edinburgh, UK.

NULL HYPOTHESIS

To test whether the distributions of independent samples in a contingency table differ significantly we begin by stating the null hypothesis that there is no difference. Since the totals for the samples in the contingency table are usually different, H_0 does not necessarily imply that the cells of each sample have the same values. Rather, H_0 implies that the value of each cell of the first sample column, as a proportion of the total for that column, equals the corresponding proportionate values for the second sample column, and equals the corresponding proportionate values for the third sample column, and so on. For example, in the 4 × 2 contingency table shown in Table 6.2, H_0 implies:

$$\frac{a}{(a+b+c+d)} = \frac{w}{(w+x+y+z)}$$

and $$\frac{b}{(a+b+c+d)} = \frac{x}{(w+x+y+z)}$$

and $$\frac{c}{(a+b+c+d)} = \frac{y}{(w+x+y+z)}$$

and $\dfrac{d}{(a + b + c + d)} = \dfrac{z}{(w + x + y + z)}$

Table 6.2 Observed values in a 4 × 2 contingency table

	Sample$_1$	Sample$_2$	Total
—	a	w	a + w
—	b	x	b + x
—	c	y	c + y
—	d	z	d + z
Total	a + b + c + d	w + x + y + z	a + b + c + d + w + x + y + z

EXPECTED VALUES

Table 6.3 shows the values for Table 6.2 expected if H_0 were true. These expected values have been denoted as a', b', and so on. The marginal totals, including the sum of all the cells $(a + b + c + d + w + x + y + z)$, remain unaltered.

Table 6.3 Values for the 4 × 2 contingency table of Table 6.2 expected under H_0

	Expected values		Total
	Sample$_1$	Sample$_2$	
—	a'	w'	a + w
—	b'	x'	b + x
—	c'	y'	c + y
—	d'	z'	d + z
Total	a + b + c + d	w + x + y + z	a + b + c + d + w + x + y + z

To calculate the expected values, we have:

a' = the proportion of $(a + b + c + d)$ expected from the first row total

$= [(a + w)/(a + b + c + d + w + x + y + z)](a + b + c + d)$

$= \dfrac{\text{(row total)} \times \text{(column total)}}{\text{sum of cells}}$

Similarly:

b' = the proportion of $(a + b + c + d)$ expected from the first row total

$= [(b + x)/(a + b + c + d + w + x + y + z)](a + b + c + d)$

$$= \frac{\text{(row total)} \times \text{(column total)}}{\text{sum of cells}}$$

Similarly:

$$c' = \frac{\text{(row total)} \times \text{(column total)}}{\text{sum of cells}}$$

and $$d' = \frac{\text{(row total)} \times \text{(column total)}}{\text{sum of cells}}$$

For sample$_2$:

w' = the proportion of $(w + x + y + z)$ expected from the first row total

$= [(a + w)/(a + b + c + d + w + x + y + z)](w + x + y + z)$

$$= \frac{\text{(row total)} \times \text{(column total)}}{\text{sum of cells}}$$

In general:

$$\text{Expected value of a cell} = \frac{\text{(row total)} \times \text{(column total)}}{\text{(sum of cells)}} \qquad (6.2)$$

CALCULATION OF χ^2

The value of χ^2 for a contingency table is calculated from the sum:

$$\chi^2 = \sum \frac{(\text{observed value} - \text{expected value})^2}{\text{expected value}} \qquad (6.3)$$

which can also be written as:

$$\chi^2 = \sum \frac{(O - E)^2}{E} \qquad (6.4)$$

where O = observed value and E = expected value.

Thus, for Tables 6.2 and 6.3, Equation 6.4 gives rise to Figure 6.4.

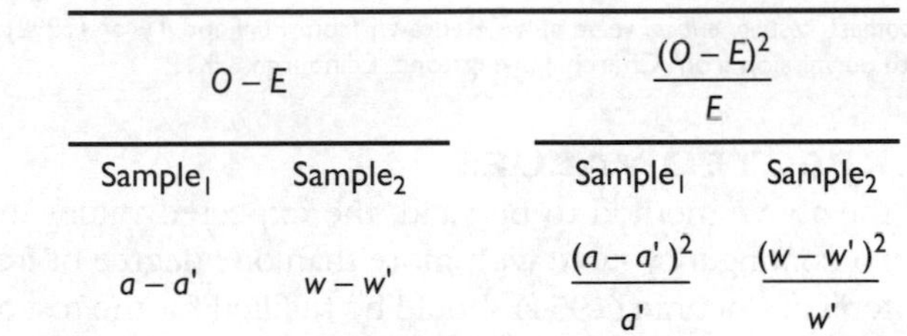

$O - E$		$\dfrac{(O - E)^2}{E}$	
Sample$_1$	Sample$_2$	Sample$_1$	Sample$_2$
$a - a'$	$w - w'$	$\dfrac{(a - a')^2}{a'}$	$\dfrac{(w - w')^2}{w'}$
$b - b'$	$x - x'$	$\dfrac{(b - b')^2}{b'}$	$\dfrac{(x - x')^2}{x'}$
$c - c'$	$y - y'$	$\dfrac{(c - c')^2}{c'}$	$\dfrac{(y - y')^2}{y'}$
$d - d'$	$z - z'$	$\dfrac{(d - d')^2}{d'}$	$\dfrac{(z - z')^2}{z'}$
Total 0	0		

These two totals are always zero

The sum of these two totals is χ^2

Figure 6.4 *Calculating χ^2. Redrawn from Puri and Tyrer (1992)* Sciences Basic to Psychiatry, *with permission from Churchill Livingstone, Edinburgh, UK.*

CRITICAL VALUE OF χ^2

For a significance level α, Table V is used to determine the critical value, χ^2_α. If the value of χ^2 for the contingency table is greater than χ^2_α then H_0 is rejected; otherwise H_0 cannot be rejected (see Figure 6.5).

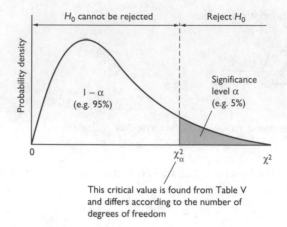

Figure 6.5   Hypothesis testing: critical value of χ^2. Redrawn from Puri and Tyrer (1992) Sciences Basic to Psychiatry, with permission from Churchill Livingstone, Edinburgh, UK.

SMALL EXPECTED VALUES

In order for the above method to be valid, the expected values must not be too small. For a contingency table with more than one degree of freedom, the following criteria of Cochran (1954) should be fulfilled for the test to be valid:

- each expected value ≥ 1
- in at least 80% of cases, expected value > 5.

If these criteria are not fulfilled, it may be possible to fulfil them by combining or omitting classes (with consequent loss of information), increasing sample size, or by using computer programs that determine exact conditional tests of independence (Agresti and Wackerly, 1977).

Example 6.2   Two independent random samples of patients with the same degree of an illness were chosen. Sample 1 consisted of 145 patients who were treated with a new drug, while sample 2 consisted of 140 patients acting as a control group. The stage of illness was classed in five categories, from considerable improvement (I) to death (V), and the results after a given period are shown in Table 6.4. Is there any difference between the two groups at the 5% level of significance?

Table 6.4 Table of observations for Example 6.2

Stage of illness	Sample 1	Sample 2	Total
I	9	19	28
II	80	75	155
III	44	33	77
IV	10	9	19
V	2	4	6
Total	145	140	285

The calculation of the expected values, based on the null hypothesis that there is no difference between the groups, is shown in Table 6.5.

Table 6.5 Calculation of expected cell values under H_0 for the data in Table 6.4

| Stage | Expected values | | Total |
	Sample 1	Sample 2	
I	14.25	13.75	28
II	78.86	76.14	155
III	39.18	37.82	77
IV	9.67	9.33	19
V	3.05	2.95	6
Total	145.01	139.99	285

The row and column totals should be the same as for the contingency table containing the original frequencies (Table 6.4). This provides a useful check if χ^2 is being calculated manually. (The slight discrepancy of 0.01 in the column totals is caused by rounding errors.) From Table 6.5 it can be seen that all the expected values are greater than 1, and that 80% are greater than 5, so that the expected values are not too small.

The calculation of $(O-E)$ is shown in Table 6.6.

Table 6.6 Calculation of $(O - E)$ for the data in Table 6.4

| | $O - E$ | | Total |
	Sample 1	Sample 2	
I	−5.25	5.25	0
II	1.14	−1.14	0
III	4.82	−4.82	0
IV	0.33	−0.33	0
V	−1.05	1.05	0
Total	−0.01	0.01	0

In Table 6.6 the row and column totals should be zero. This provides another useful check. (Once again, the slight discrepancy of 0.01 in the column totals is caused by rounding errors.) Finally, $(O-E)^2/E$ is calculated, as shown in Table 6.7.

Table 6.7 Calculation of $(O - E)^2/E$ for the data in Table 6.4

| Stage | $(O-E)^2/E$ | |
	Sample 1	Sample 2
I	1.934	2.005
II	0.016	0.017
III	0.593	0.614
IV	0.011	0.012
V	0.361	0.374
Total	2.915	3.022

From Table 6.7 the value of χ^2 can be obtained by adding the two column totals:

$$\chi^2 = 2.915 + 3.022 = 5.937$$

Using Equation 6.1, degrees of freedom = 4.

From Table V, the critical value, $\chi^2_{0.05}(4) = 9.488$.

Since $3.022 < 9.488$, we must accept the null hypothesis that there is no statistically significant difference between the two groups. This is shown in Figure 6.6.

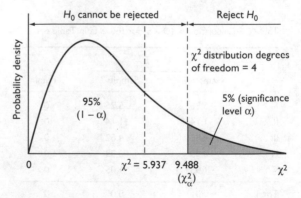

Figure 6.6 $\chi^2(4)$: the result for Example 6.2

GOODNESS-OF-FIT

The χ^2 test can be used to test how well a given distribution fits a given distribution, such as the binomial, Poisson or Normal distributions. H_0 is that the sample data follow the given distribution, and H_1 is that they do not. The frequencies expected under the given distribution are calculated and a table drawn up containing both the sample data and the values expected under H_0. These paired values are then compared using the χ^2 test. In practice, computer statistics programs usually allow the steps of such an analysis to be carried out automatically.

SPSS for Windows
See end of Chapter.

χ^2 TEST: ONE DEGREE OF FREEDOM

A contingency table has one degree of freedom when it is 2×2.

FORMULA
Using the nomenclature in Table 6.8, the following simplified formula can be used to calculate χ^2 when dealing with a 2×2 contingency table:

$$\chi^2 = \frac{(az - by)^2 (a + b + y + z)}{(a + b) (y + z) (a + y) (b + z)} \tag{6.5}$$

Table 6.8 Observed values in a 2×2 contingency table

	—	—	Total
—	a	y	$a + y$
—	b	z	$b + z$
Total	$a + b$	$y + z$	$a + b + y + z$

SMALL VALUES
All the expected values in a 2×2 contingency table need to be at least 5 in order to use Equation 6.5; therefore the overall total must be at least 20. If the total is less than 20, Fisher's exact probability test (described below) can be used.

If $20 \leq$ total < 100, then a better fit with the continuous χ^2 distribution is provided by modifying Equation 6.5 by using Yates' continuity correction:

$$\chi^2_{corrected} = \frac{\{|az - by| - \frac{1}{2}(a + b + y + z)\}^2 (a + b + y + z)}{(a + b) (y + z) (a + y) (b + z)} \tag{6.6}$$

In Equation 6.6 $|az - by|$ is the modulus of $(az-by)$ and means that the positive numerical value of $(az-by)$ is used. For example:

$$|6.4| = 6.4$$
$$|-3.14| = 3.14$$

and so on.

Although some statisticians have argued that Yates' continuity correction should be used with all 2×2 contingency tables, this is probably not necessary; a useful rule of thumb is to use it when an observed value is less than 10.

Example 6.3   Table 6.9 shows the orientation of parietal hair whorls in schizophrenic patients and normal controls (Puri *et al.*, 1995). Is the frequency distribution of hair whorl orientation significantly different between these two groups?

Table 6.9 Parietal hair whorl orientation in schizophrenia (after Puri *et al.*, 1995)

	Clockwise	Anticlockwise
Schizophrenic patients	114	12
(n = 126)	(90.5%)	(9.5%)
Normal controls	1629	261
(n=1890)	(86.2%)	(13.8%)

Since the overall total > 100, and all observed values > 10, Equation 6.5 can be used:

$$\chi^2 = \frac{((114)(261)-(1629)(12))^2(2016)}{(1743)(273)(126)(1890)]}$$
$$= 1.853$$

From Table V, the critical value, $\chi^2_{0.05}(1) = 3.841$.

Since $1.853 < 3.841$, we must accept the null hypothesis that there is no statistically significant difference between the two groups. (If Equation 6.6 (Yates' correction) is used, $\chi^2_{corrected} = 1.505$, and the result is the same.)

PROPORTIONS

A 2×2 contingency table can clearly be used to compare sample proportions. This is an alternative to using the standard error of the difference between sample proportions (Equation 5.7) in conjunction with the Normal distribution, as indicated in Chapter 5.

We saw in Chapter 4 that if W is the sum of the squares of ν independent variables, Z_1 to Z_ν, where each $Z \sim N(0, 1)$, then $W \sim \chi^2(\nu)$. It follows that for one degree of freedom:

$$\chi^2(1) = Z^2$$

Therefore, both methods give the same answer.

Equation 5.7 can be used to calculate confidence intervals when using the χ^2 test to compare proportions.

Example 6.4   Consider again Table 6.9 showing the orientation of parietal hair whorls in schizophrenic patients and normal controls (Puri *et al.*, 1995). Does the proportion of the schizophrenic patients with clockwise hair whorls differ significantly from the corresponding proportion of normal controls?

To compare the 2 sample proportions we simply apply the χ^2 test to Table 6.9 and proceed as in Example 6.3.

If, in Examples 6.3 and 6.4, the expected values had been too small to allow the χ^2 test to be used, we could instead have used Fisher's exact probability test. This is described next.

SPSS for Windows
See end of Chapter.

FISHER'S EXACT PROBABILITY TEST

This test determines exact probabilities for 2×2 contingency tables. It is not used routinely for analyzing 2×2 contingency tables with large values because its determination involves the use of factorials; factorials of large numbers are too large to be handled by calculators and personal computers. For example, $70! > 10^{100}$.

Using the nomenclature of Table 6.8, the formula used is:

$$\text{Exact probability of table} = \frac{(a + y)! \, (b + z)! \, (a + b)! \, (y + z)!}{(a + b + y + z)! \, a! \, b! \, y! \, z!} \quad (6.7)$$

In order to test H_0 : there is no difference between the samples, in addition to calculating the probability of the table we also have to calculate the probabilities of more extreme tables occurring by chance. The commonest method of doing this is illustrated in the following example.

Example 6.5   Table 6.10 shows the number of patients from two groups who are hypertensive. Is the difference between these two groups statistically significant?

Table 6.10 Hypertension in two groups of patients

	Group A	Group B	Total
Hypertensive	3	1	4
Not hypertensive	14	17	31
Total	17	18	35

The null hypothesis is that there is no difference between the two groups in the proportion who are hypertensive. We shall test H_0 at the 5% significance level ($\alpha = 0.05$).

Using Equation 6.7, the exact probability of Table 6.10 is:

$$4! \, 31! \, 17! \, 18!/(35! \, 3! \, 14! \, 1! \, 17!) = 0.2338$$

The smallest marginal total in Table 6.10 is 4, which can be made up in the following ways:

(1) $4 + 0 = 4$
(2) $3 + 1 = 4$ (this is the one in the table of observations)
(3) $2 + 2 = 4$
(4) $1 + 3 = 4$
(5) $0 + 4 = 4$

Therefore there are five ways the observed values can be arranged, keeping the marginal totals constant, as shown in Figure 6.7.

Figure 6.7   The five possible tables (keeping the marginal totals constant) for the observations in Table 6.10. Redrawn from Puri and Tyrer (1992) Sciences Basic to Psychiatry, with permission from Churchill Livingstone, Edinburgh, UK.

Add to the probability of the observed table the probabilities of more extreme tables which differ in the same direction as the observed table. Using Equation 6.7, the exact probability of the more extreme table (1) is 0.0455. So the overall probability is given by:

$$P(\text{table 2}) + P(\text{table 1}) = 0.2338 + 0.0455 = 0.279$$

(to 3 significant figures)

Since $0.279 > \alpha$, H_0 cannot be rejected. The difference between the two groups is not statistically significant at the 5% level.

SPSS for Windows
Select Statistics
        Summarize
                Crosstabs
                Enter Row and Column Variables
                Click the Statistics button and check the Chi-square box
                Continue
                OK

The Pearson chi-square value is the value of χ^2 described in this chapter.
The Continuity correction is the value with Yates' continuity correction, as described above.
The program checks if it is dealing with a 2×2 table with any expected value < 5, in which case it automatically also applies Fisher's exact probability test.

SUMMARY

- The χ^2 and Fisher's exact probability tests can be used to compare independent qualitative and discrete quantitative variables presented in the form of contingency tables containing the actual frequencies.

- The χ^2 and Fisher's exact probability tests are non-parametric (or distribution-free) tests.

- To apply the χ^2 distribution, the number of degrees of freedom, ν, of a contingency table is (number of rows-1)(number of columns-1).

- Under H_0 in the χ^2 test, expected value of a cell, E = (row total)(column total)/(sum of cells); $\chi^2 = \Sigma[(O-E)^2/E]$, where O is the observed value.

- In hypothesis testing, if the value of χ^2 for a contingency table is greater than χ^2_α then H_0 is rejected; otherwise H_0 cannot be rejected.

- For a contingency table with $\nu > 1$, the χ^2 test is valid so long as $E \geqslant 1$ (for all E) and $E > 5$ in at least 80% of cases.

■ The use of the χ^2 test (including a simplified formula) for a 2×2 contingency table ($\nu = 1$) is valid so long as $E \geqslant 5$ (for all E); otherwise Fisher's exact probability test can be used.

■ If $20 \leqslant$ total < 100 for a 2×2 table, a better fit with the continuous χ^2 distribution is provided by using Yates' continuity correction.

■ A 2×2 contingency table can be used to compare sample proportions since $\chi^2(1) = Z^2$, where $Z \sim N(0, 1)$.

■ In order to test H_0 using Fisher's exact probability test, add the probabilities of the observed table and more extreme tables (in the same direction).

EXERCISE

1 What type of data can be analysed using the χ^2 and Fisher's exact probability tests?

2 What criteria should be fulfilled in order to use the following tests to analyse a contingency table:
(a) χ^2 test
(b) Fisher's exact probability test?

3 In a study of Down's syndrome and season of birth, it was found that 100% (4/4) of the patients born in January and February were female, compared to 44% (28/63) of the other patients born during the rest of the year (Puri and Singh, 1995). Is there any significant difference in the sex ratio between those born in January/February and those born during March–December?

4 Table 6.11 is a classification of 565 patients according to their blood group and stage of illness. Test the null hypothesis that blood group and stage of illness are independent.

Table 6.11 Stage of illness and blood group for 565 patients

Stage of illness	Blood group				
	O	A	B	AB	Total
I	56	69	23	43	191
II	35	51	26	11	123
III	55	45	21	10	131
IV	21	22	11	6	60
V	10	19	15	16	60
Total	177	206	96	86	565

REFERENCES

Agresti, A. and Wackerly, D. (1977) Some exact conditional tests of independence for $r \times c$ cross-classification tables. *Psychometrika,* **42**, 111.

Cochran, W. G. (1954) Some methods for strengthening the common χ^2-test. *Biometrics,* **10**, 417-51.

Puri, B. K., El-Dosoky, A., Cheema, S., Lekh, S. K., Hall, A. D. and Mortimer, A. M. (1995) Parietal scalp hair whorl patterns in schizophrenia. *Biological Psychiatry,* **37**, 278-9.

Puri, B. K. and Singh, I. (1995) Season of birth in Down's syndrome. *British Journal of Clinical Practice,* **49**, 129-30.

CHAPTER 7

Correlation and linear regression

This chapter is concerned with sets of data involving observations of two variables, that is, bivariate data. Such data can be represented graphically in scatter diagrams. Figure 7.1 shows a scatter diagram in which the line of best fit has been drawn in. This line is called the linear regression line. Later in this chapter we will see how to determine its equation.

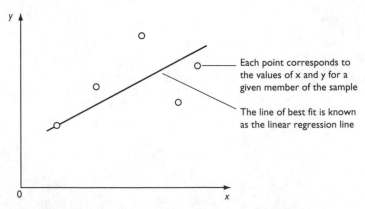

Figure 7.1   A scatter diagram of bivariate data with a linear regression line drawn in

Note that the line of best fit is not necessarily a straight line. It may be curved, as in Figure 7.2.

CORRELATION

Correlation measures the relationship for bivariate data between the two variables. If two random variables are positively correlated, they tend to increase or decrease together. If they are negatively correlated, one tends to increase as the other tends to decrease.

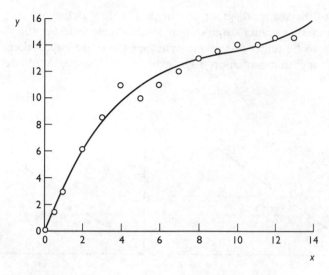

Figure 7.2   A scatter diagram of bivariate data with a curved (cubic) line of best fit

CORRELATION COEFFICIENT

The correlation coefficient is a measure of the degree of correlation. The symbol r is used to denote Pearson's product moment correlation coefficient obtained from a sample, usually referred to simply as the (sample) correlation coefficient. Its value varies between -1 and 1 (inclusive):

$$-1 \leqslant r \leqslant 1 \qquad (7.1)$$

The corresponding population correlation coefficient is denoted by the Greek letter ρ (rho). Figure 7.3 shows typical scatter diagrams for all possible values of r; a value of 1 implies perfect positive correlation, 0 implies no correlation at all, and -1 implies perfect negative correlation.

The correlation coefficient is calculated from:

$$r = \frac{\Sigma(x - \bar{x})(y - \bar{y})}{\sqrt{\Sigma(x - \bar{x})^2 \, \Sigma(y - \bar{y})^2}} \qquad (7.2)$$

From this equation it is evident that r does not have any units. Many scientific calculators allow r to be calculated by entering paired values of (x, y). After calculating r using a computer program or calculator, it is a good idea to plot the scatter diagram, to check that the calculated value of r is in the right range. A scatter diagram may also indicate whether the line of best fit is likely to be linear or curved, whether there are any outliers, and the nature of any transformation that may be necessary to obtain a linear relationship.

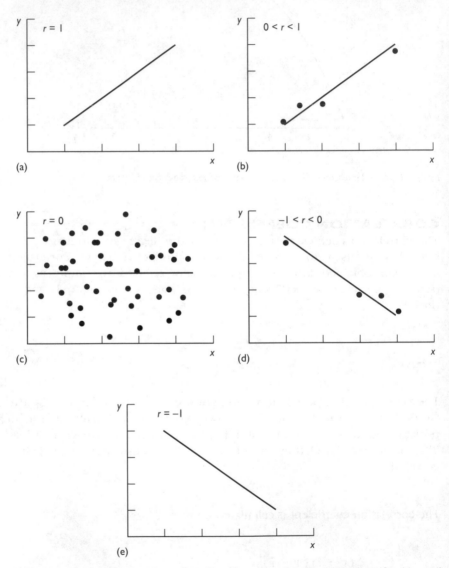

Figure 7.3   Typical scatter diagrams and linear regression lines for all possible values of r. (a) r = 1; (b) 0 < r < 1; (c) r = 0; (d) −1 < r < 0; (e) r = −1

Example 7.1   Table 7.1 shows the cerebrospinal fluid (CSF) levels of 5-HIAA (5-hydroxyindoleacetic acid) and cortisol in eight untreated depressed patients. Determine the value of the sample correlation coefficient for the two CSF substances.

Table 7.1 CSF levels of 5-HIAA and cortisol in eight untreated depressed patients

Patient	5-HIAA (nmol l⁻¹)	Cortisol (nmol l⁻¹)
1	50	27
2	100	38
3	52	25
4	48	18
5	124	29
6	112	35
7	147	26
8	167	39

As a check, the bivariate data of Table 7.1 have been plotted as a scatter diagram in Figure 7.4, from which it is clear that r is positive but less than 1, that is, $0 < r < 1$.

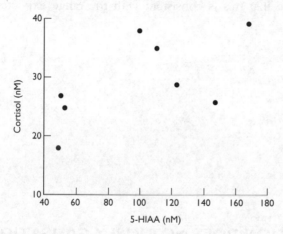

Figure 7.4 Scatter diagram of the bivariate data of Table 7.1

Omitting units, and letting x represent the CSF level of 5-HIAA and y represent the CSF level of cortisol, from the calculations shown in Table 7.2 we obtain:

$$n = 8, \Sigma x = 800, \Sigma x^2 = 94\,926, \Sigma y = 237, \Sigma y^2 = 7385, \Sigma xy = 25\,165$$

Table 7.2 Calculations on the data of Table 7.1

Patient	x	x^2	y	y^2	xy
1	50	2500	27	729	1350
2	100	10000	38	1444	3800
3	52	2704	25	625	1300
4	48	2304	18	324	864
5	124	15376	29	841	3596
6	112	12544	35	1225	3920
7	147	21609	26	676	3822
8	167	27889	39	1521	6513
Total	800	94926	237	7385	25165

Using formulae that make the manual determination of Equation 7.2 easier, we have:

$$\Sigma(x - \bar{x})(y - \bar{y}) = \Sigma xy - (\Sigma x)(\Sigma y)/n = 1465$$
$$\Sigma(x - \bar{x})^2 = \Sigma x^2 - (\Sigma x)^2/n = 14\,926$$
$$\Sigma(y - \bar{y})^2 = \Sigma y^2 - (\Sigma y)^2/n = 363.875$$

Substituting in Equation 7.2 gives:

$$r = 1465/\sqrt{[(14\,926)(363.875)]} = 0.6286$$

So the sample correlation coefficient is 0.63 to two significant figures. As a check, we note that this is consistent with the range expected from the scatter diagram.

SPSS for Windows
Select Statistics
    Correlate
        Bivariate
        Enter variables
        OK

In the Output, the top figure in each cell is r.

CORRELATION DOES NOT IMPLY CAUSATION

It is important to note that correlation does not imply causation, even in the case of perfect positive or negative correlation. You might find, for example, that the annual amount you spend on books in the years leading up to an examination is positively correlated with the annual amount spent on food over the same time. This would not imply, however, that either of these types of spending is the cause of the other. There may be indirect links between the two, such as the underlying rate of inflation in the economy generally.

INTERCHANGEABILITY OF x AND y

When one variable depends on the other, it is conventional with bivariate data to represent the dependent variable on the vertical or y-axis graphically, and the variable it depends on, the independent variable, on the horizontal or x-axis. In Equation 7.2 the values of x and y are interchangeable. In cases in which there may be a causative relationship between the two variables, r does not give any indication of which is the dependent and which the independent variable.

EXTRAPOLATION

When a linear correlation is found, it must not be assumed that r and the corresponding linear regression line can be extrapolated to encompass values of x and y outside the range used to calculate the correlation. The reason for caution is shown in Figure 7.5.

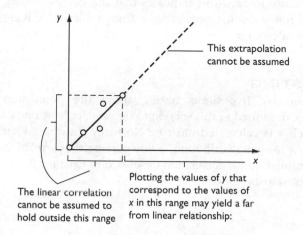

This extrapolation cannot be assumed

Plotting the values of y that correspond to the values of x in this range may yield a far from linear relationship:

The linear correlation cannot be assumed to hold outside this range

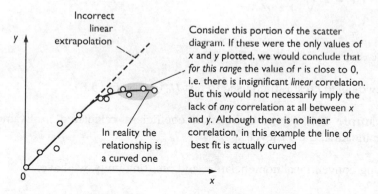

Incorrect linear extrapolation

Consider this portion of the scatter diagram. If these were the only values of x and y plotted, we would conclude that *for this range* the value of r is close to 0, i.e. there is insignificant *linear* correlation. But this would not necessarily imply the lack of *any* correlation at all between x and y. Although there is no linear correlation, in this example the line of best fit is actually curved

In reality the relationship is a curved one

Figure 7.5   *Illustration of why extrapolation may not be valid outside the range used to calculate* r

COEFFICIENT OF DETERMINATION

Consider a set of bivariate data for which there is good reason to suppose one of the variables, y say, is dependent on the other, x. Does r give any clue as to how much of the variation in the values of y is accounted for by x?

It can be shown that r^2 is the proportion of the variation in the observed values of y that can be explained by x (and therefore by the linear regression line). It is known as the coefficient of determination:

Coefficient of determination = r^2 (7.3)

From Equation 7.1 it follows that the range of r^2 is:

$$0 \leqslant r^2 \leqslant 1 \tag{7.4}$$

In addition, when r^2 is close to zero this indicates that the corresponding linear regression line is not good for predicting y from values of x lying within the range used to calculate r.

HYPOTHESIS TESTING

In order for the method of hypothesis testing about the population correlation coefficient, ρ, described in this section to be valid, at least one of the variables from which r is calculated must be Normally distributed. (If neither variable follows a Normal distribution, a non-parametric correlation coefficient, such as Spearman's rank correlation described in Chapter 9, can be used instead.) The test statistic used is:

$$t = r \sqrt{\frac{n-2}{1-r^2}} \tag{7.5}$$

The degrees of freedom $= (n-2)$.

A two-tailed t test is then used to test H_0 (see Figure 5.8).

Example 7.2 Is the correlation coefficient calculated in Example 7.1 significant at the 5% level?

Using conventional nomenclature and omitting units, we have:

$H_0 : \rho = 0$
$H_1 : \rho \neq 0$
$\alpha = 0.05$
Degrees of freedom $= n-2 = 6$
$r = 0.6286$

So, substituting in Equation 7.5, the test statistic is given by:

$$t = 0.6286\sqrt{(6/(1-0.6286^2))} = 1.980$$

From Table IV, for $\alpha = 0.05$ the critical values (two-tailed) are given by $t(6) = \pm 2.447$. Since $-2.447 < 1.980 < 2.447$, we cannot reject H_0 (see Figure

7.6); the population correlation coefficient is not significantly different from zero.

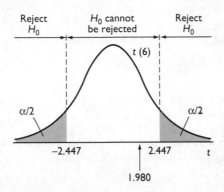

Figure 7.6   Testing H_0 in Example 7.2

SPSS for Windows
Select Statistics
    Correlate
        Bivariate
        Enter variables
        OK

In the Output, the top figure in each cell is r and the bottom figure is the two-tailed significance.

ESTIMATION OF ρ

Fisher's z transformation (Fisher, 1921) allows the sampling distribution of r, which is not Normal even if both variables are Normally distributed, to be transformed into a variable, z_r, which has an approximately Normal distribution:

$$z_r = \operatorname{arctanh} r \qquad\qquad (7.6)$$

This hyperbolic function is available on most scientific calculators. If not, the corresponding logarithmic function can be used:

$$z_r = \tfrac{1}{2} \ln\, [(1 + r)/(1-r)]$$

(ln stands for the natural logarithm, to base e.)

The estimated standard error of z_r is given by:

$$\text{Standard error of } z_r = 1/\sqrt{(n-3)} \tag{7.7}$$

Therefore, the $100(1 - \alpha)\%$ confidence interval for ρ in terms of z_r is given by:

$$z_r + z_{\alpha/2}/\sqrt{(n-3)} \text{ to } z_r + z_{1-\alpha/2}/\sqrt{(n-3)} \tag{7.8}$$

From Equation 7.6 it is clear that conversion from z_r back into r is carried out simply by using:

$$r = \tanh z_r \tag{7.9}$$

(From Equations 7.6 and 7.7 it follows that to test the null hypothesis that ρ has a value other than zero, the test statistic to use is:

$$Z = (z_r - z_\rho)\sqrt{(n-3)} \tag{7.10}$$

where $Z \approx N(0, 1)$ and $n \geqslant 25$.)

Example 7.3   Calculate a 95% confidence interval for the population correlation coefficient based on the data in Table 7.1.

We have:

$r = 0.6286$
$n = 8$
$z_{\alpha/2} = -1.96$ and $z_{1-\alpha/2} = 1.96$ (Table II)

Using Fisher's transformation (Equation 7.6):

$$z_r = \text{arctanh}\, 0.6286 = 0.739\,10$$

Substituting in Equation 7.8, in terms of z_r the 95% confidence interval is:

$$0.739\,10 - 1.96/\sqrt{5} \text{ to } 0.739\,10 + 1.96/\sqrt{5}$$
$$= -0.137\,43 \text{ to } 1.615\,64$$

Converting back to the scale used for r (Equation 7.9), the confidence interval is:

$$\tanh(-0.13743) \text{ to } \tanh 1.61564$$
$$= -0.13657 \text{ to } 0.92399$$

So the required 95% confidence interval is -0.14 to 0.92 (to 2 significant figures). (The fact that this confidence interval includes zero concurs with the result of Example 7.2.)

LINEAR REGRESSION

EQUATION OF A STRAIGHT LINE

Figure 7.7 shows that any straight line can be represented by the equation:

$$y = a + bx \tag{7.11}$$

where a is the intercept on the y-axis and b is the gradient of the line.

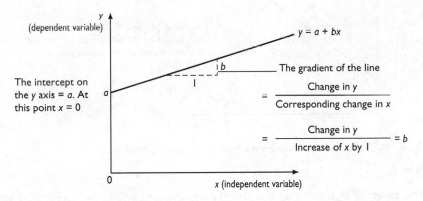

Figure 7.7   Graph of $y = a + bx$

In Figure 7.7 the gradient is positive and so b has a positive value. In Figure 7.8, however, the gradient is negative.

TRANSFORMATION

If the scatter diagram shows a non-linear relationship it may be possible to transform this into a linear relationship, for example by taking logarithms, reciprocals or square roots. Details of which transformations are worth trying are outside the scope of this book.

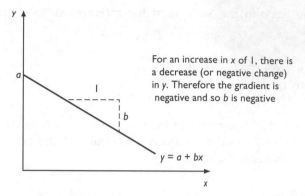

Figure 7.8   *Graph of* y = a + bx *with a negative gradient*

LINEAR REGRESSION LINE

The least squares method, illustrated in Figure 7.9, is used to calculate the values of *a* and *b* that give the straight line of best fit for bivariate data.

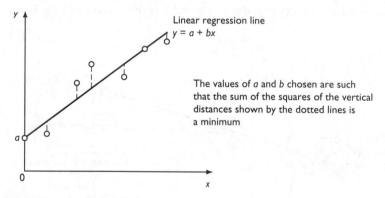

Figure 7.9   *The method of least squares to determine the linear regression line*

The value of *b*, known as the sample *regression coefficient,* yielded by this method is given by:

$$b = \frac{\Sigma(x - \bar{x})(y - \bar{y})}{\Sigma(x - \bar{x})^2} \qquad (7.12)$$

From this equation it is clear that *b* has the units of *y* divided by those of *x*. The population regression coefficient is denoted by the Greek letter β (beta).

▓ When $r > 0$, $b > 0$.

- When $r = 0$, $b = 0$ (the regression line in this case is a horizontal line intercepting the y-axis at $y = a$).
- When $r < 0$, $b < 0$.

The value of a, the intercept on the y-axis, is given by:

$$a = \bar{y} - b\bar{x} \qquad (7.13)$$

From Equation 7.13 it follows that the linear regression line passes through the mean point with coordinates $(\bar{x}, \bar{y})$.

ASSUMPTIONS

The following assumptions are made in linear regression:

- There is no error in the observed values of x.
- For any value of x, there is a Normal distribution of values of y, as shown in Figure 7.10.
- The magnitude of scatter of the values of y for each x is the same throughout the range of the linear regression line; that is, the Normal distribution curves in Figure 7.10 each have the same standard deviation.
- The true mean of y from the Normal distribution of values of y corresponding to each x lies on the linear regression line; that is, y_1 and y_2 lie on the regression line in Figure 7.10.

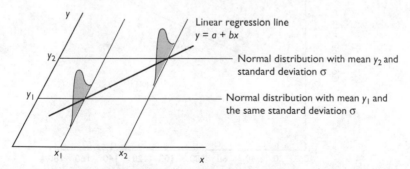

Figure 7.10 Some of the assumptions made in using linear regression. Redrawn from Puri and Tyrer (1992) *Sciences Basic to Psychiatry*, with permission from Churchill Livingstone, Edinburgh, UK.

Example 7.4 Calculate the equation of the linear regression line for the data in Table 7.1.

Omitting units, from Example 7.1 we have:

$$\Sigma(x-\bar{x})(y-\bar{y}) = \Sigma xy - (\Sigma x)(\Sigma y)/n = 1465$$
$$\Sigma(x-\bar{x})^2 = \Sigma x^2 - (\Sigma x)^2/n = 14926$$

Substituting in Equation 7.12:

$$b = 1465/14926 = 0.09815$$

Again:

$$\bar{x} = (\Sigma x)/n = 100$$
$$\bar{y} = (\Sigma y)/n = 29.625$$

Substituting in Equation 7.12:

$$a = 29.625 - (0.09815)(100) = 19.81$$

So, to 3 significant figures, the linear regression line is $y = 19.8 + 0.0982x$.

Figure 7.11 shows a scatter diagram with this linear regression line superimposed; as a useful check, ensure that the line passes through the mean point (100, 29.625).

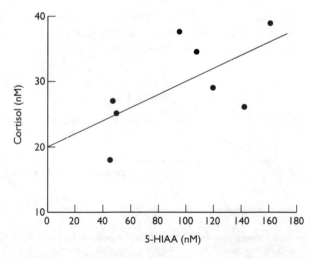

Figure 7.11   Scatter diagram of the bivariate data of Table 7.1 with superimposed linear regression line, showing that it passes through a and the mean point

PREDICTION

The linear regression line can be used to predict y for given values of x so long as the latter lie within the range of x used to calculate the linear equation, and so long as r^2 is not close to zero.

HYPOTHESIS TESTING

The variance of y about the linear regression line, $\sigma^2_{y|x}$, is estimated from $s^2_{y|x}$, which is given by:

$$s^2_{y|x} = (n - 1)(s^2_y - b^2 s^2_x)/ (n-2) \qquad (7.14)$$

where s^2_x and s^2_y are the sample variances of x and y, respectively.

To test the null hypothesis that the population regression coefficient is zero ($H_0 : \beta = 0$), the test statistic used is:

$$t = \frac{b \sqrt{\Sigma(x - \bar{x})^2}}{s_{y|x}} \qquad (7.15)$$

The degrees of freedom = $(n-2)$.

A two-tailed t test is then used to test H_0 (see Figure 5.8).

Example 7.5 Is the regression coefficient calculated in Example 7.4 significant at the 5% level?

Using conventional nomenclature and omitting units, we have:

$H_0 : \beta = 0$
$H_1 : \beta \neq 0$
$\alpha = 0.05$
Degrees of freedom = $n-2 = 6$
$b = 1465/14926 = 0.09815$
$\Sigma(x-\bar{x})^2 = \Sigma x^2 - (\Sigma x)^2/n = 14926$

From Table 7.1 we can calculate that $s^2_x = 2132.29$ and $s^2_y = 51.98$.

Substituting in Equation 7.14:

$$s^2_{y|x} = (8-1)(51.98-0.09815^2(2132.29))/ (8-2) = 36.68$$

So, substituting in Equation 7.15, the test statistic is given by:

$$t = [0.09815\sqrt{(14926)}]/\sqrt{(36.68)} = 1.980$$

From Table IV, for $\alpha = 0.05$ the critical values (two-tailed) are given by $t(6) = \pm 2.447$.

Since $-2.447 < 1.980 < 2.447$, we cannot reject H_0 (see Figure 7.6); the population regression coefficient is not significantly different from zero.

Note that the failure to reject H_0 does not necessarily imply that x and y are unrelated; alternative explanations include the possibility that the relationship between the two variables is non-linear, or that a type II error has been made.

ESTIMATION

The $100(1-\alpha)\%$ confidence intervals for β, α (the population parameter corresponding to a), and the predicted true value of y, are obtained using the two-tailed t distribution with $(n-2)$ degrees of freedom in the usual way:

$$\text{Confidence interval} = \text{statistic} + t_{\alpha/2} \text{ (standard error) to} \\ \text{statistic} + t_{1-\alpha/2} \text{ (standard error)} \tag{7.16}$$

The relevant standard errors are given by:

$$\text{Standard error of } \beta = s_{y|x}/[s_x\sqrt{(n-1)}] \tag{7.17}$$

$$\text{Standard error of } \alpha = s_{y|x}\sqrt{[(1/n) + (\bar{x}^2/(s_x^2(n-1)))]} \tag{7.18}$$

Standard error of the predicted true mean of y, for a given value of x, $x_0 = s_{y|x}\sqrt{[(1/n) + ((x_0 - \bar{x})^2/(s_x^2(n-1)))]}$ (7.19)

Example 7.6 Calculate a 95% confidence interval for the population regression coefficient based on the data in Table 7.1.

We have:

$$b = 1465/14926 = 0.09815$$
$$s_{y|x} = \sqrt{36.68} = 6.056$$
$$s_x = \sqrt{2132.29} = 46.18$$

Substituting in Equation 7.17:

$$\text{Standard error of } \beta = 6.056/[46.18\sqrt{7}] = 0.04957$$

Degrees of freedom = $n - 2 = 6$.

From Table IV, for $\alpha = 0.05$ the critical values (two-tailed) are given by $t(6) = \pm 2.447$.

So the required confidence interval is given by (Equation 7.16):

$$0.09815 - 2.447(0.04957) \text{ to } 0.09815 + 2.447(0.04957)$$
$$= -0.02314 \text{ to } 0.21945$$

So the required 95% confidence interval is -0.023 to 0.219 (to 3 decimal places). (The fact that this confidence interval includes zero concurs with the result of Example 7.5.)

SPSS for Windows

Select Statistics
    Regression
        Linear
        Enter Dependent and Independent variables
        Click Statistics button and check boxes for Confidence intervals and
        Estimates for Regression Coefficients
        Continue
        OK

Part of the Output for the analysis of the data in Table 7.1 is shown in Figure 7.12. The first row (Variable X) is b, and the second row (Variable (Constant)) is a. The second column (B) gives the values of b and a. The third column (SE B) gives their standard errors. The fourth and fifth columns (95% Confdnce Intrvl B) give the 95% confidence intervals. The next table in the Output gives the significance of b and a.

```
-------------- –Variables in the Equation --------------

Variable          B        SE B    95% Confdnce Intrvl B      Beta

X              .098151    .049573   -.023150    .219451     .628622

(Constant)19.809912    5.400009    6.596638  33.023186


--------- in ---------

Variable        T      Sig T

X            1.980    .0950

(Constant)   3.668    .0105
```

Figure 7.12   SPSS Output for linear regression analysis on data in Table 7.1

SUMMARY

- Pearson's sample product moment correlation coefficient lies in the range $-1 \leqslant r \leqslant 1$ and does not have any units.

- $r = 1$ implies perfect positive correlation, $r = 0$ implies no correlation at all, and $r = -1$ implies perfect negative correlation.

- Correlation does not imply causation.

- r does not give any indication of which is the dependent and which the independent variable.

- When a linear correlation is found, it must not be assumed that r and the corresponding linear regression line can be extrapolated to encompass values of x and y outside the range used to calculate the correlation.

- The coefficient of determination, r^2, is the proportion of the variation in the observed values of y that can be explained by x; $0 \leqslant r^2 \leqslant 1$.

- Hypothesis testing about the population correlation coefficient, ρ, using a two-tailed t test with $(n - 2)$ degrees of freedom, assumes that at least one of the variables from which r is calculated is Normally distributed.

- For the estimation of ρ, Fisher's z transformation allows the sampling distribution of r, which is not Normal even if both variables are Normally distributed, to be transformed into z_r (= arctanh r) which has an approximately Normal distribution; standard error of $z_r = 1/\sqrt{(n - 3)}$.

- A straight line can be represented by $y = a + bx$, where a = intercept on the y-axis and b = gradient of the line.

- The least squares method is used to calculate the values of a and b (the sample regression coefficient) that give the straight line of best fit for bivariate data; this line passes through the mean point $(\bar{x}, \bar{y})$.

EXERCISE

1   What do each of the following values of Pearson's product moment correlation coefficient imply?

(a) 0.25
(b) −1
(c) 0
(d) 1
(e) −0.68

2   For the data in Table 2.8 giving the elimination half-life of zopiclone and corresponding serum albumin levels in nine cirrhotic patients, calculate the following:

(a) Pearson's product moment correlation coefficient to 2 significant figures.
(b) Whether this correlation coefficient is statistically significant at the 1% level.
(c) A 95% confidence interval for the population correlation coefficient.
(d) The sample regression coefficient.
(e) The equation for the linear regression line.
(f) The predicted value of the elimination half-life when the serum albumin level is 30.0 g l^{-1}.
(g) A 95% confidence interval for the true regression coefficient.

CHAPTER 8

Analysis of variance

Analysis of variance (ANOVA) is a method that divides the total variation in a data set into components, each of which is associated with a specified source of variation, and the contribution to the total variance of these contributing sources is analysed. It will be assumed that ANOVA calculations will be carried out by computer rather than manually, since the latter can be very tedious. For this reason, details of the formulae and calculations involved will not be given in this chapter, and there is no exercise at the end of the chapter.

F TEST

In Chapter 5 we saw that when using the t distribution to compare two means, SPSS automatically checks if the variances of the two groups are significantly different, using Levene's Test for Equality of Variances, which uses the F distribution. F is the ratio of the two variances (with degrees of freedom $\nu_1 = n_1 - 1$ and $\nu_2 = n_2 - 1$, where n_1 and n_2 are the sample sizes). The closer the two variances are to each other, the closer, therefore, must F be to 1. If the calculated value of F is greater than the critical value (for given α) of $F(\nu_1, \nu_2)$, then $H_0 : \sigma_1 = \sigma_2$ is rejected.

ONE-WAY ANOVA

This is a method for comparing the means of more than two groups, and makes the assumptions that each group is an independent random sample from a Normally distributed population, and that the population variances are equal. The null hypothesis is that all the population means (and variances) are equal.

A matrix containing the sample data is analysed to give rise to a table of results in which variability between groups and within groups are compared. If the value of F is greater than the critical value of F_α, H_0 is rejected and it is concluded that all the means are not equal. This test does not, however, indicate which means are significantly different from the others. In order to determine this a multiple comparison procedure should be used, such as the Bonferroni test available in SPSS. What you must *not* do is carry out multiple t tests comparing each pair of means, as this will greatly increase the chances that you will falsely find a significant difference.

Example 8.1   A prosthesis is made out of three different materials (A, B and C). The plasticity (in arbitrary units) of a group of five samples of each material is measured. Table 8.1 shows the results. Do the plasticities of the materials differ?

Table 8.1 Plasticity of prostheses made of materials A, B and C

A	13	14	15	14	16
B	16	13	12	11	13
C	14	10	11	13	15

The data are entered into a statistics program. In the case of SPSS, the first column of Newdata can contain all 15 observations, and the second column can contain a numerical factor (1, 2 or 3) corresponding to the material used (A, B or C, respectively).

SPSS for Windows
Select Statistics
      Compare Means
            One-Way ANOVA
            Enter Dependent variable (plasticity) and Factor (type of material)
            Click Define Range button (for the Factor) and enter range (Minimum = 1, Maximum = 3)
            Continue
            OK

Figure 8.1 shows the Output ANOVA table.

Analysis of Variance

Source	D.F.	Sum of Squares	Mean Squares	F Ratio	F Prob.
Between Groups	2	8.9333	4.4667	1.4725	.2680
Within Groups	12	36.4000	3.0333		
Total	14	45.3333			

Figure 8.1   Results of a one-way ANOVA of the data in Table 8.1

> The important figures are the value of F (F Ratio), which in this case is 1.4725, and its corresponding probability (F Prob.), in this case 0.2680. Since $0.2680 > \alpha$, we cannot reject H_0 (the population means are not significantly different).

TWO-WAY ANOVA

In Example 8.1 there was only one factor to consider. If there were a second factor to consider, this would have to be taken into account as it may account for variation in the observed data, and it may itself interact with the other factor. For instance, the data in Table 8.1 may have been obtained by using five different methods to measure plasticity, as shown in Table 8.2.

Table 8.2 Plasticity of prostheses by material (A, B and C) and method of measurement (1 to 5)

Material	Method of measurement				
	1	2	3	4	5
A	13	14	15	14	16
B	16	13	12	11	13
C	14	10	11	13	15

SPSS for Windows
Select Statistics
    ANOVA Models
       Simple Factorial
       Enter Dependent variable (plasticity) and Factors (type of material and method of measurement)
       Click Define Range button (for each Factor) and enter ranges
       Continue
       OK

The SPSS output gives values of F and corresponding probabilities for each factor and for two-way interactions between the factors.

More detailed types of analysis are beyond the scope of this chapter.

SUMMARY

■ Using ANOVA the total variation in a data set is compartmentalized and the contribution to the total variance of these contributing sources is analysed.

■ In the F test, if F (= the ratio of the two variances (with degrees of freedom $\nu_1 = n_1 - 1$ and $\nu_2 = n_2 - 1$)) > $F_a(\nu_1, \nu_2)$, then $H_0 : \sigma_1 = \sigma_2$ is rejected.

■ A one-way ANOVA tests the null hypothesis that all the population means (and variances) of more than two groups are equal; it assumes that each group is an independent random sample from a Normally distributed population, and that the population variances are equal.

■ When there are two independent variables and the levels of each are combined to examine all possible combinations, a two-way ANOVA is used.

CHAPTER 9

Non-parametric and distribution-free tests

Non-parametric tests are ones that test hypotheses which do not make assumptions about the population parameters, while distribution-free tests do not make assumptions about the population distribution. In practice both terms are often treated as being equivalent. We have already met one such test, the χ^2 test, in Chapter 6.

ADVANTAGES

They have the advantage that they can be applied in more general conditions than can parametric tests. Another advantage is that if data are being analysed manually, then with sample sizes of less than about 50 these tests can be very simple to use.

DISADVANTAGES

When the assumptions required for a parametric test are met, then if a non-parametric test is used instead there is a discarding of useful information from the data. This will become evident from the examples in this chapter, in which rank or sign may be used in a non-parametric test, as opposed to the actual numerical values in the parametric equivalent.

Another disadvantage is that although it is possible to make estimations with non-parametric tests, the methods may be very tedious if carried out manually; non-parametric tests are essentially significance tests.

TYPES

The Wilcoxon rank sum test, Mann–Whitney U test, and Wilcoxon signed rank test are non-parametric equivalents of parametric tests based on the t distribution.

Similarly, non-parametric equivalents of Pearson's product moment correlation coefficient, r, include Spearman's rank correlation and Kendall's rank correlation.

The widely used χ^2 test has been described in Chapter 6.

A selection of these tests is now described.

WILCOXON RANK SUM TEST

Two samples are compared, mainly with respect to location. The test assumes the samples are independent and random; they need not be equal in size. The null hypothesis is that there is no difference in location. The related Mann–Whitney U test is very similar and is not described further.

METHOD

The observations are ranked together in ascending order. If more than one observation has the same value they are each assigned the appropriate mean rank. The sum of the ranks in the smaller group is T. If both samples have the same size, either sum can be used as T. Tables are available that allow the critical values of T to be looked up for given sample sizes n_1 and n_2. Alternatively, many computer programs can evaluate the value found automatically. If the value obtained lies outside the range defined by the critical values, H_0 is rejected (see Figure 9.1).

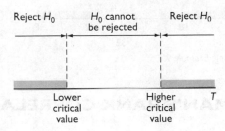

Figure 9.1   Hypothesis testing: critical value of T

Example 9.1   Table 9.1 gives the fear ratings (on a scale from 0 to 100) of two groups of patients treated differently. Do they differ?

Table 9.1 Fear ratings of two groups of patients

Group 1	Group 2
40	10
30	35
15	15
15	80
25	70
60	

Figure 9.2 shows the ranking of these data; the three observations with value 15, circled in Figure 9.2, each have the mean rank of 2nd, 3rd and 4th, namely 3rd.

Sample 1	Rank		Sample 2	Rank
40	8		10	1
30	6		35	7
(15)	3		(15)	3
(15)	3		80	11
25	5		70	10
60	9			
Total $n_2 = 6$	34		$n_1 = 5$	32

Figure 9.2   Ranking data in Table 9.1 for the Wilcoxon rank sum test

From Figure 9.2, $T = 32$.

From tables, with n_1 (smaller sample size) = 5 and $n_2 = 6$, the critical values ($\alpha = 0.05$) are 18 and 42. Since $18 < 32 < 42$, the difference between the two groups is not statistically significant at the 5% level and H_0 cannot be rejected (Figure 9.3).

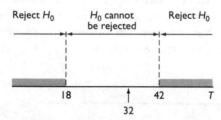

Figure 9.3   Hypothesis testing: Example 9.1

SPEARMAN'S RANK CORRELATION

This method uses the differences between pairs of ranks to give a non-parametric equivalent of r. Spearman's rank correlation, r_s, lies in the same range as r:

$$-1 \leqslant r_s \leqslant 1$$

Also, as with r:

$r_s = 1$ implies perfect positive correlation
$0 < r_s < 1$ implies fair (but not perfect) positive correlation
$r_s = 0$ implies no correlation
$-1 < r_s < 0$ implies fair (but not perfect) negative correlation
$r_s = -1$ implies perfect negative correlation

METHOD
This is illustrated with an example.

Example 9.2 Consider again the data in Table 2.8. What is Spearman's rank correlation?

The data are first ranked as in the previous example. The results of this are shown in Table 9.2.

Table 9.2 The elimination half-life of zopiclone and corresponding serum albumin levels in nine cirrhotic patients with their ranks

Patient	Serum albumin (g l^{-1})	Rank	Elimination half-life (h)	Rank
1	29.2	4	10	7
2	25.1	3	11.6	8
3	27.5	1.5	9.2	6
4	27.5	1.5	12.6	9
5	40	6	6.2	2
6	42.4	9	5.3	1
7	41.7	7	7.8	4.5
8	36.6	5	7.2	3
9	42.1	8	7.8	4.5

The difference between the ranks, d, is calculated and squared, as shown in Table 9.3.

Table 9.3 Difference between ranks, d, and d^2 for Table 9.2

Rank of serum albumin	Rank of elimination half-life	d	d^2
4	7	−3	9
3	8	−5	25
1.5	6	−4.5	20.25
1.5	9	−7.5	56.25
6	2	4	16
9	1	8	64
7	4.5	2.5	6.25
5	3	2	4
8	4.5	3.5	12.25
Total		0	213

Thus $\Sigma d^2 = 213$.

Spearman's rank correlation is calculated from:

$$r_s = 1 - \frac{6\Sigma d^2}{n(n^2 - 1)}$$ (9.1)

n = number of patients = 9.

Substituting into Equation 9.1 we have:

$$r_s = 1 - 6(213)/[9(9^2 - 1)] = -0.775$$

The significance of the above result can be assessed by using the test statistic as for r (Equation 7.5), with $(n-2)$ degrees of freedom, so long as $n \geqslant 10$. If $n < 10$, there are tables of critical values available. For our result, with $n = 9$, the critical values ($\alpha = 0.05$) are ± 0.683, which means that our result is significant at the 5% level, as shown in Figure 9.4.

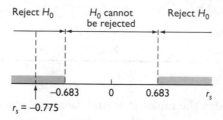

Figure 9.4   Hypothesis testing: Example 9.2

KENDALL'S RANK CORRELATION

This is similar to Spearman's rank correlation, having the same range and the same meaning (a value of 1 implies perfect positive correlation, and so on). It is denoted by the Greek letter τ (tau).

SPSS for Windows
Some non-parametric tests are available in SPSS from the following menu:
Select Statistics
        Nonparametric tests

SUMMARY

■   Non-parametric tests do not make assumptions about the population parameters.

▪ Distribution-free tests do not make assumptions about the population distribution.

▪ They can be applied in more general conditions than can parametric tests.

▪ The Wilcoxon rank sum test, Mann–Whitney U test, and Wilcoxon signed rank test are non-parametric equivalents of parametric tests based on the t distribution.

▪ Spearman's rank correlation and Kendall's rank correlation are non-parametric equivalents of Pearson's product moment correlation coefficient.

▪ The χ^2 test is a non-parametric test.

Appendix: Statistical tables

Table 1 Areas under the standard Normal distribution probability density function curve, $N(0, 1)$. This is $P(0 < Z < z)$. For $P(Z < z)$, i.e. $\Phi(z)$, add 0.5 to the value given in this table (see Fig. 4.35). (Reproduced with permission from Puri and Tyrer (1992) *Sciences Basic to Psychiatry*, Churchill Livingstone, Edinburgh.)

z	.00	.01	.02	.03	.04	.05	.06	.07	.08	.09
0.0	.0000	.0040	.0080	.0120	.0160	.0199	.0239	.0279	.0319	.0359
0.1	.0398	.0438	.0478	.0517	.0557	.0596	.0636	.0675	.0714	.0753
0.2	.0793	.0832	.0871	.0910	.0948	.0987	.1026	.1064	.1103	.1141
0.3	.1179	.1217	.1255	.1293	.1331	.1368	.1406	.1443	.1480	.1517
0.4	.1554	.1591	.1628	.1664	.1700	.1736	.1772	.1808	.1844	.1879
0.5	.1915	.1950	.1985	.2019	.2054	.2088	.2123	.2157	.2190	.2224
0.6	.2257	.2291	.2324	.2357	.2389	.2422	.2454	.2486	.2517	.2549
0.7	.2580	.2611	.2642	.2673	.2704	.2734	.2764	.2794	.2823	.2852
0.8	.2881	.2910	.2939	.2967	.2995	.3023	.3051	.3078	.3106	.3133
0.9	.3159	.3186	.3212	.3238	.3264	.3289	.3315	.3340	.3365	.3389
1.0	.3413	.3438	.3461	.3485	.3508	.3531	.3554	.3577	.3599	.3621
1.1	.3643	.3665	.3686	.3708	.3729	.3749	.3770	.3790	.3810	.3830
1.2	.3849	.3869	.3888	.3907	.3925	.3944	.3962	.3980	.3997	.4015
1.3	.4032	.4049	.4066	.4082	.4099	.4115	.4131	.4147	.4162	.4177
1.4	.4192	.4207	.4222	.4236	.4251	.4265	.4279	.4292	.4306	.4319
1.5	.4332	.4345	.4357	.4370	.4382	.4394	.4406	.4418	.4429	.4441
1.6	.4452	.4463	.4474	.4484	.4495	.4505	.4515	.4525	.4535	.4545
1.7	.4554	.4564	.4573	.4582	.4591	.4599	.4608	.4616	.4625	.4633
1.8	.4641	.4649	.4656	.4664	.4671	.4678	.4686	.4693	.4699	.4706
1.9	.4713	.4719	.4726	.4732	.4738	.4744	.4750	.4756	.4761	.4767
2.0	.4772	.4778	.4783	.4788	.4793	.4798	.4803	.4808	.4812	.4817
2.1	.4821	.4826	.4830	.4834	.4838	.4842	.4846	.4850	.4854	.4857
2.2	.4861	.4864	.4868	.4871	.4875	.4878	.4881	.4884	.4887	.4890
2.3	.4893	.4896	.4898	.4901	.4904	.4906	.4909	.4911	.4913	.4916
2.4	.4918	.4920	.4922	.4925	.4927	.4929	.4931	.4932	.4934	.4936
2.5	.4938	.4940	.4941	.4943	.4945	.4946	.4948	.4949	.4951	.4952
2.6	.4953	.4955	.4956	.4957	.4959	.4960	.4961	.4962	.4963	.4964
2.7	.4965	.4966	.4967	.4968	.4969	.4970	.4971	.4972	.4973	.4974
2.8	.4974	.4975	.4976	.4977	.4977	.4978	.4979	.4979	.4980	.4981
2.9	.4981	.4982	.4982	.4983	.4984	.4984	.4985	.4985	.4986	.4986
3.0	.4987	.4987	.4987	.4988	.4988	.4989	.4989	.4989	.4990	.4990

Table II Two-tailed percentage points for the standard Normal distribution, $N(0, 1)$ (see Fig. 4.46). (Reproduced with permission from Puri and Tyrer (1992) *Sciences Basic to Psychiatry*, Churchill Livingstone, Edinburgh.)

α	z
0.5	0.67
0.1	1.64
0.05	1.96
0.01	2.58
0.001	3.29

Table III One-tailed percentage points for the standard Normal distribution, $N(0, 1)$ (see Fig. 4.47). (Reproduced with permission from Puri and Tyrer (1992) *Sciences Basic to Psychiatry*, Churchill Livingstone, Edinburgh.)

α	z
0.5	0
0.25	0.67
0.1	1.28
0.05	1.64
0.025	1.96
0.01	2.33
0.005	2.58
0.001	3.09
0.0005	3.29

Table IV Two-tailed t distribution with $v = n-1$ degrees of freedom, $t(v)$ (see Fig. 4.49). (Reproduced from Fisher and Yates (1963) Statistical Tables for Biological, Agricultural and Medical Research, Longman.)

v	.9	.8	.7	.6	.5	.4	.3	.2	.1	.05	.02	.01	.001
												Probability	
1	.158	.325	.510	.727	1.000	1.376	1.963	3.078	6.314	12.706	31.821	63.657	636.619
2	.142	.289	.445	.617	.816	1.061	1.386	1.886	2.920	4.303	6.965	9.925	31.598
3	.137	.277	.424	.584	.765	.978	1.250	1.638	2.353	3.182	4.541	5.841	12.924
4	.134	.271	.414	.569	.741	.941	1.190	1.533	2.132	2.776	3.747	4.604	8.610
5	.132	.267	.408	.559	.727	.920	1.156	1.476	2.015	2.571	3.365	4.032	6.869
6	.131	.265	.404	.553	.718	.906	1.134	1.440	1.943	2.447	3.143	3.707	5.959
7	.130	.263	.402	.549	.711	.896	1.119	1.415	1.895	2.365	2.998	3.499	5.408
8	.130	.262	.399	.546	.706	.889	1.108	1.397	1.860	2.306	2.896	3.355	5.041
9	.129	.261	.398	.543	.703	.883	1.100	1.383	1.833	2.262	2.821	3.250	4.781
10	.129	.260	.397	.542	.700	.879	1.093	1.372	1.812	2.228	2.764	3.169	4.587
11	.129	.260	.396	.540	.697	.876	1.088	1.363	1.796	2.201	2.718	3.106	4.437
12	.128	.259	.395	.539	.695	.873	1.083	1.356	1.782	2.179	2.681	3.055	4.318
13	.128	.259	.394	.538	.694	.870	1.079	1.350	1.771	2.160	2.650	3.012	4.221
14	.128	.258	.393	.537	.692	.868	1.076	1.345	1.761	2.145	2.624	2.977	4.140
15	.128	.258	.393	.536	.691	.866	1.074	1.341	1.753	2.131	2.602	2.947	4.073
16	.128	.258	.392	.535	.690	.865	1.071	1.337	1.746	2.120	2.583	2.921	4.015
17	.128	.257	.392	.534	.689	.863	1.069	1.333	1.740	2.110	2.567	2.898	3.965
18	.127	.257	.392	.534	.688	.862	1.067	1.330	1.734	2.101	2.552	2.878	3.922
19	.127	.257	.391	.533	.688	.861	1.066	1.328	1.729	2.093	2.539	2.861	3.883
20	.127	.257	.391	.533	.687	.860	1.064	1.325	1.725	2.086	2.528	2.845	3.850
21	.127	.257	.391	.532	.686	.859	1.063	1.323	1.721	2.080	2.518	2.831	3.819
22	.127	.256	.390	.532	.686	.858	1.061	1.321	1.717	2.074	2.508	2.819	3.792
23	.127	.256	.390	.532	.685	.858	1.060	1.319	1.714	2.069	2.500	2.807	3.767
24	.127	.256	.390	.531	.685	.857	1.059	1.318	1.711	2.064	2.492	2.797	3.745
25	.127	.256	.390	.531	.684	.856	1.058	1.316	1.708	2.060	2.485	2.787	3.725
26	.127	.256	.390	.531	.684	.856	1.058	1.315	1.706	2.056	2.479	2.779	3.707
27	.127	.256	.389	.531	.684	.855	1.057	1.314	1.703	2.052	2.473	2.771	3.690
28	.127	.256	.389	.530	.683	.855	1.056	1.313	1.701	2.048	2.467	2.763	3.674
29	.127	.256	.389	.530	.683	.854	1.055	1.311	1.699	2.045	2.462	2.756	3.659
30	.127	.256	.389	.530	.683	.854	1.055	1.310	1.697	2.042	2.457	2.750	3.646
40	.126	.255	.388	.529	.681	.851	1.050	1.303	1.684	2.021	2.423	2.704	3.551
60	.126	.254	.387	.527	.679	.848	1.046	1.296	1.671	2.000	2.390	2.660	3.460
120	.126	.254	.386	.526	.677	.845	1.041	1.289	1.658	1.980	2.358	2.617	3.373
∞	.126	.253	.385	.524	.674	.842	1.036	1.282	1.645	1.960	2.326	2.576	3.291

Table V χ^2 distribution with ν degrees of freedom, $\chi^2(\nu)$ (see Figure 4.50). For odd values of ν between 30 and 70 the mean of the tabular values for $(\nu-1)$ and $(\nu+1)$ may be taken. For larger values of ν, the expression $[(2\chi^2)^{1/2}-(2\nu-1)^{1/2}]$ may be used as a Normal deviate with $\sigma^2 = 1$, so long as it is noted that the probability for $\chi^2(\nu)$ corresponds to that of a single tail of the Normal curve. (Reproduced from Fisher and Yates (1963) Statistical Tables for Biological, Agricultural and Medical Research, Longman.)

ν	.99	.98	.95	.90	.80	.70	Probability .50	.30	.20	.10	.05	.02	.01	.001
1	.0³157	0.³628	.00393	.0158	.0642	.148	.455	1.074	1.642	2.706	3.841	5.412	6.635	10.827
2	.0201	.0404	.103	.211	.446	.713	1.386	2.408	3.219	4.605	5.991	7.824	9.210	13.815
3	.115	.185	.352	.584	1.005	1.424	2.366	3.665	4.642	6.251	7.815	9.837	11.345	16.266
4	.297	.429	.711	1.064	1.649	2.195	3.357	4.878	5.989	7.779	9.488	11.668	13.277	18.467
5	.554	.752	1.145	1.610	2.343	3.000	4.351	6.064	7.289	9.236	11.070	13.388	15.086	20.515
6	.872	1.134	1.635	2.204	3.070	3.828	5.348	7.231	8.558	10.645	12.592	15.033	16.812	22.457
7	1.239	1.564	2.167	2.833	3.822	4.671	6.346	8.383	9.803	12.017	14.067	16.622	18.475	24.322
8	1.646	2.032	2.733	3.490	4.594	5.527	7.344	9.524	11.030	13.362	15.507	18.168	20.090	26.125
9	2.088	2.532	3.325	4.168	5.380	6.393	8.343	10.656	12.242	14.684	16.919	19.679	21.666	27.877
10	2.558	3.059	3.940	4.865	6.179	7.267	9.342	11.781	13.442	15.987	18.307	21.161	23.209	29.588
11	3.055	3.609	4.575	5.578	6.989	8.148	10.341	12.899	14.631	17.275	19.675	22.618	24.725	31.264
12	3.571	4.178	5.226	6.304	7.807	9.034	11.340	14.011	15.812	18.549	21.026	24.054	26.217	32.909
13	4.107	4.765	5.892	7.042	8.634	9.926	12.340	15.119	16.985	19.812	22.362	25.472	27.688	34.528
14	4.660	5.368	6.571	7.790	9.467	10.821	13.339	16.222	18.151	21.064	23.685	26.873	29.141	36.123
15	5.229	5.985	7.261	8.547	10.307	11.721	14.339	17.322	19.311	22.307	24.996	28.259	30.578	37.697
16	5.812	6.614	7.962	9.312	11.152	12.624	15.338	18.418	20.465	23.542	26.296	29.633	32.000	39.252
17	6.408	7.255	8.672	10.085	12.002	13.531	16.338	19.511	21.615	24.769	27.587	30.995	33.409	40.790
18	7.015	7.906	9.390	10.865	12.857	14.440	17.338	20.601	22.760	25.989	28.869	32.346	34.805	42.312
19	7.633	8.567	10.117	11.651	13.716	15.352	18.338	21.689	23.900	27.204	30.144	33.687	36.191	43.820
20	8.260	9.237	10.851	12.443	14.578	16.266	19.337	22.775	25.038	28.412	31.410	35.020	37.566	45.315
21	8.897	9.915	11.591	13.240	15.445	17.182	20.337	23.858	26.171	29.615	32.671	36.343	38.932	46.797
22	9.542	10.600	12.338	14.041	16.314	18.101	21.337	24.939	27.301	30.813	33.924	37.659	40.289	48.268
23	10.196	11.293	13.091	14.848	17.187	19.021	22.337	26.018	28.429	32.007	35.172	38.968	41.638	49.728
24	10.856	11.992	13.848	15.659	18.062	19.943	23.337	27.096	29.553	33.196	36.415	40.270	42.980	51.179

Table V *continued*

ν	.99	.98	.95	.90	.80	.70	Probability .50	.30	.20	.10	.05	.02	.01	.001
25	11.524	12.697	14.611	16.473	18.940	20.867	24.337	28.172	30.675	34.382	37.652	41.566	44.314	52.620
26	12.198	13.409	15.379	17.292	19.820	21.792	25.336	29.246	31.795	35.563	38.885	42.856	45.642	54.052
27	12.879	14.125	16.151	18.114	20.703	22.719	26.336	30.319	32.912	36.741	40.113	44.140	46.963	55.476
28	13.565	14.847	16.928	18.939	21.588	23.647	27.336	31.391	34.027	37.916	41.337	45.419	48.278	56.893
29	14.256	15.574	17.708	19.768	22.475	24.577	28.336	32.461	35.139	39.087	42.557	46.693	49.588	58.302
30	14.953	16.306	18.493	20.599	23.364	25.508	29.336	33.530	36.250	40.256	43.773	47.962	50.892	59.703
32	16.362	17.783	20.072	22.271	25.148	27.373	31.336	35.665	38.466	42.585	46.194	50.487	53.486	62.487
34	17.789	19.275	21.664	23.952	26.938	29.242	33.336	37.795	40.676	44.903	48.602	52.995	56.061	65.247
36	19.233	20.783	23.269	25.643	28.735	31.115	35.336	39.922	42.879	47.212	50.999	55.489	58.619	67.985
38	20.691	22.304	24.884	27.343	30.537	32.992	37.335	42.045	45.076	49.513	53.384	57.969	61.162	70.703
40	22.164	23.838	26.509	29.051	32.345	34.872	39.335	44.165	47.269	51.805	55.759	60.436	63.691	73.402
42	23.650	25.383	28.144	30.765	34.157	36.755	41.335	46.282	49.456	54.090	58.124	62.892	66.206	76.084
44	25.148	26.939	29.787	32.487	35.974	38.641	43.335	48.396	51.639	56.369	60.481	65.337	68.710	78.750
46	26.657	28.504	31.439	34.215	37.795	40.529	45.335	50.507	53.818	58.641	62.830	67.771	71.201	81.400
48	28.177	30.080	33.098	35.949	39.621	42.420	47.335	52.616	55.993	60.907	65.171	70.197	73.683	84.037
50	29.707	31.664	34.764	37.689	41.449	44.313	49.335	54.723	58.164	63.167	67.505	72.613	76.154	86.661
52	31.246	33.256	36.437	39.433	43.281	46.209	51.335	56.827	60.332	65.422	69.832	75.021	78.616	89.272
54	32.793	34.856	38.116	41.183	45.117	48.106	53.335	58.930	62.496	67.673	72.153	77.422	81.069	91.872
56	34.350	36.464	39.801	42.937	46.955	50.005	55.335	61.031	64.658	69.919	74.468	79.815	83.513	94.461
58	35.913	38.078	41.492	44.696	48.797	51.906	57.335	63.129	66.816	72.160	76.778	82.201	85.950	97.039
60	37.485	39.699	43.188	46.459	50.641	53.809	59.335	65.227	68.972	74.397	79.082	84.580	88.379	99.607
62	39.063	41.327	44.889	48.226	52.487	55.714	61.335	67.322	71.125	76.630	81.381	86.953	90.802	102.166
64	40.649	42.960	46.595	49.996	54.336	57.620	63.335	69.416	73.276	78.860	83.675	89.320	93.217	104.716
66	42.240	44.599	48.305	51.770	56.188	59.527	65.335	71.508	75.424	81.085	85.965	91.681	95.626	107.258
68	43.838	46.244	50.020	53.548	58.042	61.436	67.335	73.600	77.571	83.308	88.250	94.037	98.028	109.791
70	45.442	47.893	51.739	55.329	59.898	63.346	69.334	75.689	79.715	85.527	90.531	96.388	100.425	112.317

Answers

CHAPTER 1

1 to 3 See text

4 (a) interval; (b) ratio; (c) ratio; (d) ordinal; (e) ratio; (f) nominal

---

CHAPTER 3

9 (a) mean = 15.1 g dl^{-1} (e) second decile (D$_2$) = 14.3 g dl^{-1}
   (b) median = 15.3 g dl^{-1} (f) interquartile range = 1.4 g dl^{-1}
   (c) mode = 14.7 g dl^{-1} (g) standard deviation = 1.0 g dl^{-1}
   (d) range = 3.8 g dl^{-1} (h) variance = 1.0 g^2 dl^{-2}

STATISTICS FOR THE HEALTH SCIENCES

150

CHAPTER 4

1 (a) $13/52 = 1/4$
   (b) $1-1/4 = 3/4$ (using Equation 4.3 for complementary events)

2 These are mutually exclusive events, therefore (using Equation 4.5):
   $P(\text{throw} = 1, 2 \text{ or } 4) = P(\text{throw} = 1) + P(\text{throw} = 2) + P(\text{throw} = 4)$
   $= 1/6 + 1/6 + 1/6 = 1/2$

3 In each trial, throwing the 3 dice are independent events. Therefore (using Equation 4.7):
   $P(\text{throw}=6 \text{ and } 6 \text{ and } 6)=P(\text{throw}=6)\times P(\text{throw}=6)\times P(\text{throw}=6)$
   $= 1/6 \text{ x } 1/6 \text{ x } 1/6 = 1/216$
   Therefore, over 1000 trials, expected number = 1000/216 = 4.6, or 5 to the nearest integer

4 3 628 800

5 Using Equation 4.9, $^{10}P_5 = 10!/5! = 30\,240$

6 Using Equation 4.10, $^{10}C_5 = 10!/(5!5!) = 252$

7 We have: number of trials = 6, $P(\text{throwing a six}) = 1/6$
   If X is the number of 'sixes' thrown, then $X \sim B(6, 1/6)$
   Using Equation 4.12, $P(X = 2) = {}^6C_2 (1/6)^2(5/6)^4 = 0.201$

8 $\sqrt{4} = 2$

10 Let the random variable be denoted by X. Then $X \sim N(75, 4^2)$.
    If $Z = (X-75)/4$, then $Z \sim N(0, 1)$.
    $\therefore P(76.1 \leqslant X \leqslant 77.0) = P((76.1-75)/4 \leqslant Z \leqslant (77.0-75)/4)$
    $= P(0.275 \leqslant Z \leqslant 0.5)$
    $= 0.1915 - 0.108\,35$ (from Table I)
    $= 0.083$ to two significant figures

11 a, b, e and h

CHAPTER 5

8 Standard error of mean = 8.64
Degrees of freedom = 24
$t(24) = 2.064$
95% confidence interval for μ = 186 to 222 μU l^{-1}

9 Observed proportion = 0.893 = 89.3%
Standard error of the proportion = 0.0356
Using the Normal distribution, the 95% confidence interval for the
true proportion = 0.823 to 0.963 = 82.3 to 96.3%

10 $H_0 : \mu_1 = \mu_2$
$H_1 : \mu_1 \neq \mu_2$
$\alpha = 0.05$
Degrees of freedom = $n_1 + n_2 - 2 = 126$
Difference between sample means = 0.9
Standard error of difference = 0.292
Test statistic, $t = 4.89$
Critical values are given by $t(126) = \pm1.98$
Since $4.89 > 1.98$, we reject H_0 at the 5% level of significance. (In
fact, from Table IV we see that $P < 0.001$). We conclude that the
mean age in the study by Puri *et al.* (1995c) is significantly greater
than that in the study by Bullock *et al.* (1990).
95% confidence interval for the true difference = 0.32 to 1.48 years.

CHAPTER 6

3 Fisher's exact test, $P = 0.047$
Therefore females were significantly more likely than males to be
born during January or February.

4 $\chi^2 = 38.53$
$\chi^2_{0.05}(12) = 21.026$
Since $38.53 > 21.026$, we reject the null hypothesis and conclude
that blood group and stage of illness are not independent ($P <
0.001$ from Table V).

CHAPTER 7

2 (a) −0.87

(b) $t = -4.56$, $\nu = 7$

Reject $H_0 : \rho = 0$; the sample correlation coefficient is statistically significant at the 1% level

(c) $z_r = -1.313\,07$, standard error of $z_r = 0.408\,25$

95% confidence interval = −0.971 to −0.472

(d) $b = -0.2897$ h g^{-1}

(e) $a = 18.68$ h

Linear regression line equation is $y = 18.68 - 0.2897x$

(f) 10.0 h

(g) standard error of $\beta = 0.063\,507$

Required confidence interval = −0.440 to −0.140 h g^{-1}

Index